WHERE?
PLACE IN RECENT
NORTH AMERICAN FICTIONS

THE DOLPHIN

General Editor: Tim Caudery

20

WHERE?
PLACE IN RECENT
NORTH AMERICAN FICTIONS

Edited by Karl-Heinz Westarp

AARHUS UNIVERSITY PRESS

General Editor: Tim Caudery

Editorial address:
The Dolphin
Department of English, Aarhus University
DK-8000 Aarhus C

Distribution:
Aarhus University Press
Building 170, Aarhus University
DK-8000 Aarhus C
Fax: + 45 86 19 70 33

ISSN 0106-4487
The Dolphin no. 20, spring issue 1991
Subscription price for one year (two issues):
Europe 198 DKK, overseas US$ 38.00.
Single copy price (not including postage):
Europe 118 DKK, overseas US$ 19.65.
Back issues available - list sent on request.

Contents

Acknowledgements

I wish to thank Patrick Lane for allowing us to publish his poem 'Indian Tent Rings', which he originally dedicated to Northrop Frye. I should also like to express my gratitude to all contributors for making their manuscripts readily available without any form of remuneration. In the production process Connie Relsted and Signe Frits showed great expertise and patience in preparing the manuscripts and their lay-out. I should also like to thank Tim Caudery, the general editor of *The Dolphin*, for his meticulous and helpful reading of the manuscripts.

We could not have published the volume without a generous grant from the University of Aarhus Research Foundation.

Karl-Heinz Westarp

Preface

'How the Self, Which Usually Experiences Itself as Living Nowhere, is Surprised to Find that it Lives Somewhere', is one of Walker Percy's subtitles in *Lost in the Cosmos*. Surely, we all know our place, know of the many different connotations of place – at least subconsciously. Yet our physical and existential form of being in time and space is never certain, always changing and often full of questions. Frederick Turner speaks about the 'spirit of place' which informs every single individual and which must reach a reflected level of consciousness to prevent uprootedness, restlessness and alienation.

In the literatures of the two North American 'nations of nations', Canada and the United States, a search for 'place' and the identification with it has been 'topological'. In their literary tradition some writers have searched back to their pre-immigration roots; others, such as for example Walt Whitman and William Carlos Williams, sought identification with their new environment, borne by the conviction that art must be bred of a place.

The search for a proper 'where' to identify with seems to be a predominant theme in recent North American literature, and the present volume of essays tries to trace the expression of this theme both in general terms and in terms of single authors. David Kranes outlines in the opening essay the crucial co-ordinates of place in general and their representation in the theatrical space in particular. James McClintock follows the works of Gary Snyder which describe the painful but necessary way back to the original roots of living on the North American continent. Finding a way back to America's ethnic roots is one objective of Native American literature, examples of which are presented by Richard E. Fisher. Darlene Erickson demonstrates that Toni Morrison is a good example of the fact that there is also a strong Black search for place in North America. The importance of the search for place in French-Canadian literature is discussed in Ellen Munley's study of the physical and metaphysical dimensions in Anne Hébert's *Les enfants du sabbat*. Jupp Schöpp analyses Raymond Federman's most recent novel, which outlines the possibilities for 'replacement' in a post-holocaust era. The same era is discussed by Regine Rosenthal in her essay about William Styron's highly controversial novel *Sophie's Choice*. The last three essays deal with expression of place in writers of the

7

American South. Karl-Heinz Westarp discusses existential displacement as typical of Flannery O'Connor's characters. Jan Nordby Gretlund takes his starting point in Eudora Welty's famous essay on place and shows how she transforms her views in one of her short stories. In the last essay Karl-Heinz Westarp tries to follow Walker Percy's fiction, in which the highly concrete places of the American South are always diaphanous for deeper and universal layers of place and displacement.

I hope that, in spite of its limited selection of authors, the present collection gives a true and stimulating picture of the presentation of place and placelessness in recent North American fictions.

Karl-Heinz Westarp
Århus, February, 1991.

Indian Tent Rings

(for Northrop Frye)

I

There is nothing here of use, only the spare
grasses bent to wind. Cattle wander through
this place, faces bred to dullness,
mouths vague machines in flesh, cropping
the thin spears. Dust, dirt, hard grasses,
dessicated moss, the stunned explosions
of lichen moving slow as startled novas
on the rocks. This land has never known a plow
yet the isolated ranchers love this place.
It is as perfect as they want it to be.
Driving in trucks they cruise this earth
in search of coyotes to run down or antelope
to push beyond the limits of their blood,
until they fall against the walls of wire
begging for an end to running.

II

I am left with stone rings as if they were
the one image I can endure. It is why
I move towards grace
and this too is a kind of endurance.
It is the image of them breaks me.
These tent rings grow on the hills
as if a living dust had been ground into them
making a proud flesh. Or is it they rise
slowly out of time like teeth
in the mouth of a dead man
that push through the leather of his lips
until they've consumed their own mask.
As if, as if ...

III

A man and a woman walk these hills. I see them
small against the cold falling down from the north.
Their eyes have wandered this prairie, praising
the natural disorder of ravines, the rare stands
of stunted poplar, the quick hurt of the dawn.
Perhaps it is only accident they find themselves
far from their city. I know they are no longer
sure of the images they were trained to believe.
The roots of Stonehenge, the grave circle at Mycenae,
the mortuary house at Leubingen are their history.

The circles lie like crucibles on the land.
The woman squats silent in a ring.
In spite of what she believes, her body is
animal. Her face is turned from the wind.
She wants to have been here since the sun was
born. Below her on the slopes the man is searching
for something, a broken arrowhead, a fractured
scraper, some sign to prove he was here.

It matters that they search for what
they do not understand. Europe is a place
they've never seen but they believe it more
than they believe this place. It is *like*,
they say. But *like* what? What brought them here?
A betrayal of concern? The flaw of freedom.
No, nothing is ever simple. Perhaps it is enough,
they are here, the woman caught in the ancient
circle and the man circling below her, his eyes
trying to find a thing that is more than
an idea, a bit of pebble carved into himself.

Patrick Lane

10

Space and Literature:
Notes Toward a Theory of Mapping

David Kranes

I can take any empty space and call it a bare stage. A man walks across this empty space whilst someone else is watching him, and this is all that is needed for an act of theatre to be engaged.[1]

We find ourselves living in something often called the 'Space Age'. I talk to a friend who tells me she's been 'spaced out'. Buckminister Fuller finds a convenient metaphor in what he calls 'This spaceship, Earth'. 'Far out!' was a '60s clichéd cry of pleasure. Psychologists talk of 'ego boundaries'. *Space* – as a word, as a concept, as a metaphor, as a dream, as a physical reality – surrounds us. Samuel Beckett's image of humanity which 'gives birth astride the grave' may be bleak, but it compresses a curve of space many believe they trace: starting from the small, protected, personal space of the womb; being delivered and falling through the air of a huge and vulnerable universal space into another closed, small personal space of earth: from womb, through space, to tomb. And one of Beckett's later plays, 'A Piece of Monologue', opens with a similar image/thought: 'Birth. Birth was the death of him'.

Another vision – more religiously, or cosmically inclined – might trace the curve from tomb back again one additional step as returning to more infinite universal space. At any rate, we exist in space. We define ourselves, orient ourselves, by varying space. We generate through space. We act and move in space. And of all literary forms, drama is clearly the most spatial. We shall here explore various ways in which space defines, forms, and conceptually, emotionally and sensually affects the dramatic experience.

Perhaps the best beginning to this material is to attempt to take the above Beckett quote into the realm of diagram – in order that it might illustrate one of the central questions and images:

What this diagram attempts to bring into early consideration and focus is the idea of *three primary spaces*. These spaces are at the centre of almost every serious literary work and I suppose every serious religion. In the centre is the life space, 'Home'. And on either side of that ... the spaces which are on either side of life – one before, one after: Womb and Tomb. These are spaces which are topologically similar. They are small spaces. They are unlit spaces. They are very enclosed spaces. Are they, then, *secure* spaces? At any rate, they are natural and unavoidable. There is no question that a given womb is the womb of its inhabiter. Death and the tomb seem almost equally unarguable spaces. Yet many feel they know much more about the vast 'Home' space between. Is that true? Are we, in fact, more 'at home' in the space of life which is between our birth and our death? Or is the space of 'Home', finally, the most insecure, unsettling, problematic crucial space of all? How one inhabits 'home' seems a critical question – in our lives, in the plays that seek to be searching images for our lives. 'Am I at home?' 'Is this my home?' 'Do I belong to this place? these people?' 'Can I rest here?' 'If I could only be dead.' 'If I had never been born.'

'Home' it would seem, then – the space of home around one ... physically, metaphysically – is the problem. How do any of us inhabit meaningfully ... intimately ... naturally ... securely?

How do any of us come to know or define or experience space in our lives? Once we have left the sure, protective, embracingly bounded, nourishing spaces of the womb, how do we come to *know*, and thus relate to, the space of the World and Universe we discover ourselves in so that we might best, in Arthur Miller's terms, 'make, of the outside World, a home'?

Two basic models for 'knowing' present themselves. The first is Euclidean, quantitative, geometric. The second is qualitative and 'topologic'. In the first, space is dealt with as a physical reality: measured, shaped, described. The second approach posits space as a phenomenon, something experienced.

Is there one of these two ways that is 'natural' to the creatures that we are? Is there one of these two ways that is learned, imposed? By the end of this section, I'll pose answers to these questions. But the questions must first be filtered through the *two models of knowing space* mentioned above. And even before describing the two models more completely, some documentation should be given to the importance of any human's *knowing* space(s) in his/her existence.

Each single, real thing bears witness to its reality above all by occupying a segment of space from which it excludes everything else.[2]

In *The Phenomenology of Knowledge*, Ernst Cassirer argues strongly in Chapter Three, 'Space', for the above point: 'There is no field of philosophy or theoretical knowledge in which the problem of space does not in some way enter and with which it is not interwoven in one way or another'. Cassirer connects this quest to know space with the ultimate attainment of an individual's 'spiritual reality'.

There is no achievement or creation of the spirit which is not in some way related to the world of space and which does not in a sense seek to make itself at home in it. ... Space forms ... the universal medium in which spiritual productivity can first establish itself, in which it can produce its first structures and formations. ... What makes a province spatially distinct is not some abstract, geometrical determination but the unique mythical atmosphere in which it stands – the magical aura that surrounds it.[3]

Once again, in trying to document the importance of spatial knowledge for the human creature, let me cite the central and definitive book *The Child's Conception of Space* by Jean Piaget. In the preface of this humane and extraordinarily researched book, Piaget states without equivocation that: 'It is clear that if the development of various aspects of child thought can tell us anything about the mechanism of intelligence and the nature of human thought in general, then the problem of space must surely rank as of the highest importance'.[4]

Let's return then – acknowledging that knowing the space(s) of our lives is critical to any of us – to the first possible model for knowing space: the quantitative model, or what has been called in philosophical terms the 'Descartes' or 'Rationalist' model. Descartes speaks directly about it: 'Every act of spatial perception comprises an act of measurement and thus of mathematical inference'.

Following this approach, we know our world by parsing it, by doling it out, by taking a tape measure to it. Asked the question: 'What is your home like?' the Cartesian Rationalist might be likely to respond: 'It is a living area of 1234 square feet. There are three bedrooms, two baths. The master bedroom is fifteen feet by twelve feet. There are two stories, 617 square feet on each story...' etc. Space for such a person would be matter of size, volume, function.

And it might well be argued that, on a shrinking planet, a planet 'housing' larger and larger numbers of people, dwellings, industries, etc., that the person who has come to know and understand space rationally, geometrically, in the way Descartes describes it, would be invaluable. Such a person can solve the problem: 'How can we accommodate a population of 350,000 Hispanics in seven square blocks on the West Side?' Figure out how much space is available overall. Figure how many people will probably fill it. Divide it up reasonably equally with perhaps some considerations for status, time of life, etc. This, in fact, is the basis for a great deal of contemporary applied architecture.

Before leaving this approach, it should be pointed out that, at base, this model for knowing space appears to assume it to be homogeneous: that in any given thousand-square-foot area of space, any ten-foot square section is the same as any other. They are different points on a grid or map. Verticality and horizontality have little importance. Their value is equal. Put a bed in one and a bath in the other, and they begin to differ ... functionally.

The second model for knowing space – by *topos* – is subjective and experimental. The philosophical connection is Berkeley, and the approach might be/(has been) called 'Empiricist'. This approach would posit that humans 'know' space through sense memory and through *association*, not measurement. We see and are seen in a particular space. We touch and are touched in a particular space. We experience different phenomena in particular spaces and our knowledge of those spaces comes through the associations of those experiences. All space is not equivalent or homogeneous in this approach/model. Knowledge of space, in the 'empiricist' model 'reveal[s] no absolutely homogeneous, unlimited extension, free from all sensuous qualities'. It is not through measurements and volumes that we know space in this model at all, but through *our minds, our interiors*: 'And activity ... of the imagination ... habit and custom ... combine the particular sensory spheres and finally make them grow together into such a concrete whole that they can mutually represent one another'.[5]

Ask the 'Topologist' what his/her home is like, and the response might begin: 'The room where I sleep is dark, with lots of things that make shapes. One wall hums. My bed is cold underneath, but soft and fuzzy on top. When I get out of it, to go and open my door, the floor feels prickly...' etc. In this scheme the facts of knowledge are sensory, personal. Large volumetric rooms can feel small. Tiny volumetric rooms can feel huge. The Empiricist solving the Hispanic population problem might be less practical

14

than the Rationalist. Certainly, though, his solution would involve elements to make the individual populations feel more at home, feel less restless. And it could be argued that a less restless population might 'inhabit' a given limited area more productively and happily than a 'restless' population of the same size in a larger area.

Is one of these two models more real? More natural? Less artificial than the other? The evidence – argued most sensitively and specifically by Piaget – would seem to say *yes*. It is the *topos* of space which makes critical difference to the lives of human beings. Delivered from womb into the almost overwhelming spaces of Life and World, it appears most true that our indelible knowledge of various spaces, our patterns for inhabiting well or badly, come to us through sensually experiencing – in the process of our growth, child to adult – the spaces which unfold ... in front of us, behind us, to the sides of us, beneath us, above us. We grope, see, listen, taste the dimensions around us.

In our early moments of knowing and attempting to know space, the following sorts of questions/considerations are primary:

– *How close* is anything else in space? ... That we might need? ... That might endanger us? How proximate?

– *How separated* are we in our living space? ... from others, danger, assistance, the outside, the dark, etc.?

– *Is the space ordered?* And this does not question, necessarily, geometric order. More accurately, it asks if the space has a design, an arrangement that is felt, perceived. Does the space have some sort of 'living shape'?

– *Is the space enclosed?* And this is a question that cuts two ways. Enclosure can be felt as security. And it can be felt as denied freedom, imprisonment.

Piaget makes the case clearly and eloquently for the *experienced* knowledge of space as being a deeper and far more indelible knowledge than the *measured* knowledge of space.

One question in particular invited enquiry. Geometry primers are almost unanimous in presenting the fundamental ideas of space as resting upon Euclidean concepts such as straight lines, angles, squares, circles, measurements, and the like. And this view would appear to derive support from studies in perception of visual and tactile

'Gestalten'. On the other hand, abstract geometrical analysis tends to show that fundamental spatial concepts are not Euclidean at all, but 'topological'. That is to say, based entirely on qualitative or 'bi-continuous' correspondences involving concepts like proximity and separation, order and enclosure. And indeed, we shall find that the child's space, which is essentially of an active and operational character, invariably begins with this simple topological type of relationship long before it becomes protective or Euclidean.[6]

Since 'Topology' may be a new, and for our purposes *special* word, it might be wise to cite Piaget again for a definition of it:

TOPOLOGY: is therefore basically the study of homeomorphisms; that is to say, spatial equivalences other than those of size and shape. The subject matter of topology is not distance, angle or straightness, but the property of *being connected* or *bounded*. Such a geometry does not distinguish between circles, ellipses or polygons, nor between cubes and spheres.
The most important property dealt with by topology may be said to be *proximity*.

We shrink or grow in space according to how proximate we feel another entity (harmful or enriching) to be to us. We become active or passive in space according to how proximate another such entity/person/place/object/ light etc. may be. We feel impotent or potent in space according to the same considerations of proximity. 'Nearer, my God, to Thee' expresses a topological, spatial, proximate sense of strength and fullness.

And it is *topos* which informs the central notions of two principal theorists about space – Mercia Eliade and Gaston Bachelard.

In Eliade's 'Sacred Space and Making The World Sacred', he describes the *act of cosmosgeny*. Wandering within homogeneous space, a modal world without form, the searching individual discovers or situates a sacred space. He marks it. He marks it by driving an *axis mundi* into the earth, a *vertical axis* which articulates three realms of existence and becomes their center. The *axis mundi* projects itself *up* into the spirit world of the heavens; it projects itself *down* into the dark and unknown spirit underworld; in doing so it intersects the third plane, that plane upon which man walks. So in Eliade's sacred topos there is a *center*, an *axis mundi*, connecting man to spirit realms of dark and light. From this axised center there radiates the sacred circle, the circumference of which *bounds* the sacred space. Within the space, man feels empowered; without the space, all becomes modal again, homogeneous, formless. The temple is at the center. Beyond the defining walls, beyond the gate lies the world of 'other' rather than 'brother'. A horizontal axis within the circle connects brother to brother; it is the social axis where the vertical is the spiritual axis.

16

Bachelard in his *Poetics of Space* outlines the same topology for the *oneiric self*, the positive day dreamer. There is the hearth. There is the *axis mundi* reaching into the attic (that place of reflection and memory) and down into the basement (that place of the unconscious and of night dreaming with its damp walls and earthen floor). Bachelard gives us poetic images of windows and doors – across which thresholds and through which glass we experience the *dialectic of inside and outside.*

Both writers, in their topological analyses of space, invite us to remember those moments when we have felt empowered, 'centerd', rooted because we have been in a true *home* or because we have lived – tribally or personally – within a sacred space. And conversely, they invite us to recall those often terrifying moments when – with the elements of center, axis, circle, borders, thresholds absent – we have felt unformed and dissolved in our lives, minds and spirits.

In our reading, then, we may begin to read differently once we begin to notice the force of these topological considerations on characters, to test the relative truth of these two models on them – their problems, their attempted solutions.

In focusing on a text as a spatial reality, there are a number of considerations and questions which may be of value to pursue. The following questions/considerations are hardly exhaustive. Still they may provide certain guidelines, perhaps a pattern of approach. These questions/considerations fall into three broad areas: (1) a description of the space; (2) central characters' *attitude* toward the space; (3) action and movement within the space. In short, the first area addresses itself to the space itself, the second connects character to that space, and the third some interaction of the two: space and character. These considerations apply basically to the illusionistic space: where the play is *supposed* to take place.

A. Description of the Space:

1. *Is it a bounded or unbounded space?* Is the space defined by boundaries or limits? The answer will generally be *yes.* If the answer is yes, *why* are the boundaries there? What do they wall in, wall out? What are they (illusionistically) made of? Is this significant?

2. *Is it a geometric or ungeometric space?* In considerations of visual art geometry is often associated with a classical approach and lack of geometry

(biomorphic form) with a more organic, romantic, even gothic approach. Within this question a second question might occur: *is it a symmetric or asymmetric space?* Is symmetry or balance an important element in terms of character? or emotions? or the reality? or the theme?

3. *Is it a centered (focused) or uncentered (unfocused) space?* Within the space where the dramatic action occurs, does there seem to be some spot or point or focus which has dramatic significance? For example, some character might associate being in such a spot, point, focus as the achievement of some center-focus-clarity-stability within him/herself. In her wonderful book, *Centering*, Mary Richards states: 'A potter brings his clay into center on the potter's wheel, and then he gives it whatever shape he wishes. ... The center holds us all, and as we speak out of it, we speak in common voice.'

4. *Is it an ordered or unordered space?* This applies really to the contents of the space (objects, furniture, props, etc.). Does the placement and arrangement seem to indicate order or disorder? Is it planned or random? Is it methodic or chaotic? Does the order or lack thereof in the space seem significant?

5. *Is it a closed or open space?* This applies really to the first question about boundaries. The basic question here is does the space have access? Can freedom be gained out of it or into it? Is *passage* in all senses – physical, emotional, literary – possible into or out of this space?

6. Related to above: *is it a compressive or expansive space?* Does it seem to generate a force which presses in or pushes out? Does it seem personally/ emotionally crushing or explosive? Does it seem to be trying to be smaller or larger than it actually is?

7. *Is it an objective or subjective space?* This focuses on the basic level of reality. In a basically realistic work, the space would be objective – a space in which bodies move. In a dream reality, the space would be subjective – a space in which the mind moves. Strindberg, in defining this type of theatre, in his preface to *A Dream Play*, states that 'over all – is the consciousness of the dreamer'.

8. *Is it a public or private place?* This is usually very central to the action: echoing or conflicting strongly with central characters and their attempted actions. Some examples:

Public Places	Private Places
Offices	One's *own* room
Meeting rooms	bedrooms
Court rooms	studies
City squares	dens
Cafés	
Public streets	
(within one's house)	
living rooms	
sitting rooms	
dining rooms	

9. *What surrounds the space (beyond boundaries)?* Dark? Sunrise? Rain? Cold? Revolution?

B. Central Characters' Attitudes Toward the Space(s)

1. *Do important characters have a basically positive or negative attitude towards the space?* This is not to suggest an always clear-cut attitude. Often we inhabit spaces which we feel ambivalent about. If this should be true in a given work, is it possible then to isolate what aspects (areas) of the total space trigger negative feelings? A character, for instance, might love the furnishings (contents) but hate the structure (package). This is another of the more critically important questions relating to space and its use. A lot flows from solid answers to this.

2. *Is it a familiar or unfamiliar space?* Does the character seem to know the space rather well? Could he find his way around it with the lights out? Does this familiarity (or lack of it) seem a comfort or a burden? Familiarity can be a source of security or boredom. Unfamiliarity can excite fear or adventure.

3. Related to both the above: *Does the space seem to dominate the character, or does the character seem to dominate the space?* Again, this is not always clear-cut. Perhaps most often, it is a dynamic during the play, that is, an element which changes: man begins by dominating his space; this leads, perhaps, to overbearing pride; a *hubric* error of judgement is made; and man ends in a space which dominates him. *Oedipus*'s final space is blindness, the dark – and he is dominated by it.

C. Movement, Action, Change, Progression of Character(s) Within the Space

Physically a standing character has six choices of movement: up, down, left, right, forward, backward. Or he may stand still and not move. These patterns become enlarged and sometimes symbolic in the study of dramatic events.

1. *Does the character have a basically static or kinetic relationship to the space?* What does the physically static image of a person frozen in space signify? Is he 'frozen'? 'Paralysed'? Contemplative? At rest? Patient? Is his *stasis* a refusal or an acceptance? The same questions should be applied to *kinesis* within a space, or into a space, or out of a space. What does the motion ultimately mean? Frenzy? Joy? Confusion? Distraction?

2. *How are the principle motions best characterized?*

   (a) *Habitual?* Is the character simply caught up in the formed pattern of his life and responding, moving, acting rather automatically? Is it the movement of a programmed or conditioned body – separate from its will or mind?

   (b) *Ritualistic?* Like habitual movement, this would be highly patterned, even predictable, but it would also have purpose. It would have an agreed-upon significance. It would most likely be communal – anywhere from the ritual of two lovers and its private significance to the ritual of a religious congregation and its community significance. The element of *significant* movement, action, etc., being *agreed-upon* is, I think, important here.

   (c) *Explorative?* (forward): Is discovery an objective of the movement? Does a character move across a space or act within it to find out? Does the exploration have positive or negative motivation? Is it for enlightenment? understanding? dominance? rape? possession? invasion? penetration? love? fulfilment?

   (d) *Withdrawal?* (backward): Again motivation here is of central importance. One may back off, withdraw out of deep compassion or equal cowardice. The body may withdraw so that the mind might explore and discover. The mind may withdraw so that the body may power ahead without thought or guilt.

(e) *Ascent or descent?* When Aristotle describes one aspect of tragedy as the 'fall of someone in high position' he uses spatial and kinetic terms in his metaphor. Irony may be a factor: what on the outside may look like a character's rising may, on the inside, be his decline. Macbeth, in seeking high office, descends morally. Were the play to be examined on a physical, staging level, motion up and down could be seen as enriching the thematic metaphor.

(f) *Regular or irregular movement?* (flexible and inflexible): Regularity can indicate authority or it can indicate rigidity. Irregularity might mean indecision or flexibility.

(g) *Socially accepted or unaccepted?* Certain movements, actions, etc., in given spaces meet with general approval, others become odd or defiant or asocial.

None of what has been introduced above should be taken in isolation. This is of critical importance. The three major areas of description of space, attitude toward space, action and movement within space lock together. The questions within and across the areas interlock. Combined, they provide a partial system to study literary and dramatic texts spatially.

What is most important is the pattern that, taken together, these various elements begin to illuminate and reveal.

NOTES

1. Peter Brook, *The Empty Space* (New York: Avon Books, 1968), p. 9.
2. Ernst Cassirer, *The Phenomenology of Knowledge* (New Haven: Yale University Press, 1957), p. 143.
3. Cassirer, op. cit., p. 144.
4. Jean Piaget and Bärbel Inhelder, *The Child's Conception of Space* (New York: W.W. Norton & Company, 1967), p. vii.
5. Cassirer, op. cit., p. 145.
6. Piaget & Inhelder, op. cit., Translator's note, Preface, p. vii.

Gary Snyder
and Re-inhabiting Place

James I. McClintock

City of buds and flowers
Where are your fruits?
Where are your roots. –
           'For Berkeley'

Pulitzer Prize winning American poet, essayist, and environmental activist Gary Snyder does not accept conventional political descriptions and divisions of place. His own northern California homestead address as it has appeared in print does not have a post office zip code. It is 'Shasta Nation, Turtle Island, Third Planet out from the Sun,' or it is 'Watershed: west slope of the northern Sierra Nevada, south slope of the east-west running ridge above the south fork, at the level of Black oak mixed with Ponderosa pine'.[1] He has *re*-inhabited this place because it was originally inhabited by Native Americans and later logged and burned by turn of the century entrepreneurs. Such addresses not only acknowledge that Indians once inhabited his place but also the natural features and ecological realities of the land surrounding him. Snyder writes in the introductory note to his best known volume of poems and essays, *Turtle Island*,[2] that 'The "U.S.A.", and its states and counties are arbitrary and inaccurate impositions on what is really here'. 'Turtle Island' is a better 'address' because it is the Indian name for North America linked to 'creation myths of people living here for millennia'; and such a name allows us to 'see ourselves more accurately on this continent of watersheds and life-communities – plant zones, physiographic provinces, culture areas; following natural boundaries' (TI, unpaginated).

    The most widely respected and often quoted geographers, such as Yi-fu Tuan, Edward Relph, and James Houston have convinced other geographers what is common sense for most of us – that mere space is not place. Houston, for instance, states:

Space ... has no meaning other than a mathematic one ... Place, on the other hand, has a human context: space with historical associations where vows are made; encounters and obligations, met; commitments fulfilled; limits recognized. Place implies belonging. It establishes identity. It defines vocation. It envisions destiny. Place is filled with memories of life that provide roots and give direction.[3]

Gary Snyder would agree with these humanist geographers as far as they go, but he argues for a yet more encompassing humanism that would 'include the nonhuman' – plant-life, animals, even mountain ranges, as well as human beings ('Wilderness', TI, pp. 107-108).

This not-so-common-sensical viewpoint has gained acceptance among the environmentally active during the past three decades and is, now, a cornerstone of environmental activism. The vows made, obligations met, commitments fulfilled, limits recognized and roots established and honored occur ideally in a human community that is integrated with nature.

The problem has been, of course, that vows and commitments have been broken, limits ignored, and roots severed. In our century a body of writing has emerged about dis-placement and placelessness – the loss of identity, of cultural memory, of disrupted connections between people and the land. Its philosopher is Martin Heidegger and its most powerful symbolic expression is T. S. Eliot's 'The Wasteland'. From Gary Snyder's earliest poems and essays in *Myths & Texts*, and *Earth House Hold*, to Pulitzer Prize winning *Turtle Island*, the interviews and essays in *The Real Work*, and recent poetry in *Axe Handles* and *Left Out in the Rain*,[4] he has written both in anger and sorrow about loss of place as social and spiritual issues and pointed to underlying causes in industrial capitalism, in the Judeo-Christian tradition, in greed, arrogance and ignorance. Anger and sorrow permeate the following poem from the 'Logging' section of the poem sequence entitled *Myths & Texts*:

```
The Groves are down
          cut down
Groves of Ahab, of Cybele
Pine trees, knobbed twigs
     thick cone and seed
     Cybele's tree this, sacred in groves
Pine of Seami, cedar of Haida
Cut down by the prophets of Israel
     the fairies of Athens
     the thugs of Rome
          both ancient and modern;
```

```
Cut down to make room for the suburbs
Bulldozed by Luther and Weyerhaeuser
Crosscut and chainsaw
        square heads and finns
        high-lead and cat-skidding
Trees down
Creeks choked, trout killed, roads.
Sawmill temples of Jehovah.
Squat black burners 100 feet high
Sending the smoke of our burnt
Live sap and leaf
To his eager nose.
```
                                                    ('Logging', M&T, #14)

There can be no escaping the land's ruination. For Americans who think they can escape the reality of landscape ravaged and culture dehumanized by finding their Walden Pond or 'lighting out for the territory' Snyder notes:

> I'll say this real clearly, because it seems that it has to be said over and over again: There is no place to flee to in the U.S. There is no 'country' that you can go and lay back in. There is no quiet place in the woods ... The surveyors are there with their orange plastic tape, the bulldozers are down the road warming up their engines, the real estate developers have got it all on the wall with pins in it, the county supervisors are in the back room drinking coffee with the real estate subdividers ... and the forest service is just about to let out a big logging contract to some logging company.
>
> ('The *East West* Interview', RW, p. 118)

Gary Snyder is not simply, however, another American Jeremiah or poet of placelessness and dis-placement. He has become the most articulate spokesperson for the positive vision of 'Re-inhabiting' place and affirming a 'bioregional' perspective. In an essay entitled 'Re-Inhabitation', he refers to

> the tiny number of persons who come out of the industrial societies ... and then start to turn back to the land, to place. This comes for some with the rational and scientific realization of inter-connectedness, and planetary limits. But the actual demands of a life committed to place ... are so physically and intellectually intense, that it is a moral and spiritual choice as well.[5]

To re-inhabit a place, one must have an ecological perspective that affirms interconnectedness and acknowledges limits, a perspective that extends beyond the intellectual to an ethical and spiritual vision. Beyond anger and sorrow, Snyder has faith in that cultures will eventually emerge from people who share commitments to places and who honor their roots.

24

Snyder's ideas are reflected by Kirkpatrick Sale in *Dwellers in the Land: The Bioregional Vision* (1985).[6] 'To become dwellers in the land ... the crucial and perhaps only and all-encompassing task is to understand *place*' (p. 42). We must begin by 'knowing the land' (p. 44) or, as Snyder exhorts us in the poem 'For the Children', we must *'learn the flowers'* (TI, p. 86). As he writes elsewhere, 'You should know what the complete natural world of your region is and know what all its interactions are and how you are interacting with it yourself. This is just part of the work of becoming who you are, where you are' (*'Road Apple* Interview', RW, p. 16).

Knowing the land is always, for Snyder, experiential. One must know the land with 'one's body, commitment, time, labor, walking' ('On Earth Geography', RW, p. 23). But above and beyond the directly experiential encounter with nature, with the manzanita plants, flickers, deer, and mountain ridges which fill his poetry, is knowledge of land that is intellectual. Snyder understands nature's activity as he has been taught by, among others, ecologists Howard T. Odum and his better known and widely admired brother Eugene Odum, ecologist-conservationist Raymond Dasmann, and Spanish ecologist Ramon Margalef.[7] Their lessons are now familiar to educated people: nature is a series of communities of complexly interdependent organisms that are linked by the food chain; and mature ecosystems are at 'climax' state when balanced between maximum stability and maximum diversity. As Snyder summarizes in a mid-seventies essay, 'The Politics of Ethnopoetics,' amidst references to Eugene Odum and Ramon Margalef:

Life moves in certain kinds of cycles, and after an occasion of disruption or turbulence, it rapidly replaces the disturbed fabric, but initially with a small number of species. As the fabric is repaired, species diversity begins to replace single species rapid growth, and increasing complexity becomes again the model, what they call 'tending toward climax' resulting in the condition called climax. That is, maximum diversity and maximum stability in a natural system. Stable because there are so many interlocking points that one kind of ... insult to the system does not go through too many pathways, but is localized and corrected.

(OW, pp. 28-29)

Snyder is especially fascinated by these ecologists' discussions of the flow of energy through ecosystems and of energy storage through feedback mechanisms. Stored energy is referred to as 'information'. As the Spanish ecologist Ramon Margalef, whom Snyder calls a genius, writes, 'the development of the meanders in a river, the increasing complexity of the earth's crust through successive epochs of orogenesis, are information-storing devices in the same manner that genetic systems are' (PET, pp. 3-4). 'The treasure of life', Snyder writes 'is the richness of stored information in the diverse genes of all living beings' ('Energy is Eternal Delight', TI, p. 103). Paraphrasing Eugene Odum, Snyder writes,

> Life-biomass ... is stored information; living matter is stored information in the cells and in the genes ... there is more information of a higher order of sophistication and complexity stored in a few square yards of forest than there is in all the libraries of mankind. Obviously, that is a different order of information. It is information of the universe we live in. It is the information that has been flowing for millions of years.
>
> ('Wilderness', TI, pp. 107-108)

Snyder is attracted to the writings of ecological writers not only because they provide a scientific account of nature's operations but because words such as 'community,' 'energy,' and 'information' are loaded with human significance. To know the workings of nature is to come to know more profoundly the workings of society and the possibilities of culture. To Snyder the appeal of the Odum brothers, Margalef, Dasmann and others is that their nature discussions lead them to draw conclusions about mechanisms of cultural development that underscore the importance of place.

Snyder has learned that 'certain human societies have demonstrated the capacity to become mature in the same way' as natural systems, to reach a 'climax state' in which stability is achieved with diversity and wisdom ('*East West*,' RW, p. 116). Our contemporary industrial civilizations are not examples of cultures in the climax state; in fact, ours are highly unstable, wasteful 'monocultures' (RW, pp. 116-117). Ironically, the 'only societies that are mature', Synder concludes, 'are primitive societies' populated by 'people of place' (RW, p. 116).

Hence the second injunction after 'know the flowers' for re-inhabiting place is to 'know the lore' which entails discovering how earlier communities lived in that place, not so we can imitate them literally but to learn from them wisdom we have lost. To recover wisdom is so important Snyder once said if he were recommending anything to university students to study above all else, it would be 'biology or anthropology'. 'Anthropology is probably the most intellectually exciting field in the universities' ('The Real Work', RW, p. 58). He, himself, had written an undergraduate thesis, later published, about a Haida Indian myth; and, certainly, native American lore is central to much of his finest poetry – especially in *Myths & Texts*.[8]

In seeking to define his own northern California region, Snyder says the most useful beginning was to correlate two kinds of maps: one showing California locations of the 'original Indian culture groups and tribes (culture areas)' superimposed on other maps locating watersheds and other ecological features ('On Earth Geography', RW, p. 24). Another device for beginning to learn the lore is to 'throw out a European name' of a place (as he has in substituting 'Turtle Island' for North America) ('Real Work', RW, p. 69). It can be done anywhere in America: 'Learn about Cincinnati ... Get rid of the name *Cincinnati* ... because after all it's the Ohio River Valley, really, that you're looking at. And *Ohio* means *beautiful* in [the] Shawnee [language]. And there you go, you start going back and connecting with all those loops' ('The Real Work', RW, p. 59). Links will be forged between past and present. Even city dwellers will learn about links to natural settings and earlier peoples. Cities in most cases were 'tribal marketplaces' at the 'mouths of rivers, or at fords on rivers – hence *Ox*ford University. Or they will find that their city was the goal of religious pilgrimage to a sacred place such as Jerusalem' ('Real Work', RW, pp. 69-70).

Snyder agrees with anthropologist Stanley Diamond, whose works he has read, including *In Search of the Primitive*, that 'the sickness of civilization consists in its failure to incorporate (and only then) to move beyond the limits of the primitive'.[9] To Snyder, the following modern social and political lessons can be drawn from knowledge of the practices of primitive 'inhabitory people':

1. We can have neighborhoods and communities 'strong in their sense of place, proud and aware of local and special qualities' ('Poetry, Community & Climax', RW, p. 161).

2. Environmental responsibility comes from people who work and live together in their place ('Poetry, Community & Climax', RW, p.161). This will help contemporary environmentalism advance. Quoting bioregionalist Peter Nabokov, Snyder reports that 'good-hearted environmentalists can turn their back on a save-the-wilderness project when it gets too tiresome and return to a city home. But inhabitory people will 'fight for their lives like they've been jumped in an alley'.[10]

3. 'Rootedness' will move people to make changes, even revolutionary ones, in the ways they organize their politics and economies – they will move towards decentralized, steady-state economies as farming practices and business practices become harmonious with ecological circumstances. The Pueblo Indian societies, like other primitive groups, 'practiced a kind of ultimate democracy' in which 'plants and animals are also people ... and given a place and a voice' in politics through ritual and dance ('Energy', TI, p. 104).

Perhaps the most important lesson to be learned from studying the 'lore' is how primitives united wild nature and culture through religious belief and spiritual practice. The most important benefits of place can be spiritual.

Although nineteenth century Romantics re-sacralized wilderness, Snyder argues that 'very old place centered cultures' go beyond a romantic 'vague sense of the sacred' to speak to us about 'sacred groves, sacred land' within a 'context of genuine belief and practice' ('Good, Wild, Sacred', p. 10). In 'this poem is for bear' Snyder uses Native American myths, embued with religious beliefs. The poem's language is indebted to Indian ritual chants which express the interdependency between a sacralized wild nature and the human:

this poem is for bear

"As for me I am a child of the god of the mountains."

A bear down under the cliff.
She is eating huckleberries.
They are ripe now
Soon it will snow, and she
Or maybe he, will crawl into a hole
And sleep ... .

The others had all gone down
From the blackberry brambles, but one girl
Spilled her basket, and was picking up her
Berries in the dark.

A tall man stood in the shadow, took her arm,
Led her to his home. He was a bear.
In a house under the mountain
She gave birth to slick dark children
With sharp teeth, and lived in the hollow
Mountain many years.
        snare a bear: call him out:
honey-eater
forest apple
light-foot
Old man in the fur coat, Bear! come out!
Die of your own choice! ... .

Then the poem ends with a comic acknowledgement on Snyder's part of his distance from primitive hunting and spiritual skill, that in the twentieth century his fantasy about being an Indian hunter is a bit silly:

– I think I'll go hunt bears.
        'hunt bears?
Why shit Snyder,

You couldn't hit a bear in the ass
with a handful of rice!'.

('Hunting', M&T, #6)

In many essays from 'Poetry and the Primitive' (1969) in *Earth House Hold* to 'Good, Wild, Sacred' (1983) in *CoEvolution Quarterly*, Gary Snyder has repeatedly outlined his *credo* that 'places take us out of our little selves into the larger self of the whole universe' ('Good, Wild, Sacred', p. 16). To have a true sense of place is to live in the sacred. While he is a disciplined, practicing Buddhist, Snyder argues that we can learn from Native American traditions, as well as Buddhism, how to get out of our 'little selves'. These ancient traditions combine with modern ecological science which has been

laying out (implicitly) a spiritual dimension. We must find our way to seeing the mineral cycles, the water cycles, air cycles, nutrient cycles, as sacramental – and we must incorporate that insight into our own personal spiritual quest and integrate it with all the wisdom teachings we have received from the ... past.

('Reinhabitation', OW, p. 63)

Our goal, Snyder believes, must be to integrate and absorb the 'most imaginative extensions of science' as well as 'primitive ... models of ... nature related cultures' and to 'build a community where these two vectors cross' ('Four Changes', TI, p. 102). Native Americans and Buddhists share in the wisdom traditions by both having inherently ecological understandings of the interdependencies and equality of all living and non-living 'citizens' of nature, and by both practicing rituals that lead them to contact with the 'Original Mind'. Original mind is, of course, an abstract conception, but it is essentially that state of awareness which is free from presuppositions and is untarnished by narrow secular religious education. In the traditions I have mentioned, all things epxress Original Mind – not only humans and animals but also plants and, even, rocks and the earth.

A group's holy man or shaman, whether Indian Medicine man or Buddhist teacher, has access to Original Mind. Through ritual dance and story, he brings the contents of external wilderness, its wild creatures, and internal wilderness, the unconscious, into culture and there reconciles them. Through tribal rituals of dance and song, everyone shares in the Original Mind and lives in a sacralized nature and community. Snyder's interest in Shamanism is long standing – beginning as early as his undergraduate thesis, which employs his reading of Joseph Campbell's studies of myth and Carl Jung's interpretation of archetypes to discuss the shaman's trance and dream journey as a way to make conscious and public the unconscious knowledge of his primitive community's members.[11] Shamanism is often mentioned in essays collected in *The Real Work*.

Snyder, of course, has long understood and sought to explain the essential likeness of the shaman and the poet. Poems at their best, he believes, come from Original Mind ('The Real Work', RW, p. 79). In words that should be applied to Snyder, himself, he writes that the shaman poet is 'simply the man whose mind reaches easily out into all manners of shapes and other lives, and gives song to dreams' ('Poetry and the Primitive', EHH, p. 122). And he acts both as surrogate Indian Medicine man in a poem like '*this is for bear*' and Buddhist teacher who, from another angle of vision, expresses Original Mind.

Snyder is no dilettante in Buddhist spiritual discipline, having spent a total of almost ten years as a practicing Buddhist monk in Japan and having become an important figure in American Buddhism. Buddhist teaching is apparent in poems such as 'Avocado':

The Dharma is like an Avocado!
Some parts so ripe you can't believe it,
But it's good.
And other places hard and green
Without much flavor,
Pleasing those who like their eggs well-cooked.

And the skin is thin,
The great big round seed
In the middle,
Is your own Original Nature –
Pure and smooth,
Almost nobody ever splits it open
Or ever tries to see
If it will grow.

Hard and slippery,
It looks like
You should plant it – but then
It shoots out thru the
            fingers –
gets away.

(TI, p. 61)

The two guises of Buddhist teacher and Indian medicine man are merged into many less obviously spiritual poems, for example, 'The Flickers' poem from the 'Little Songs for Gaia' section of *Axe Handles*, a volume of poetry whose setting in his place in the Sierra foothills:

THE FLICKERS

sharp call

THIS!

THIS!

THIS!

in the cool pine breeze.

(AxH, p. 57)

The flicker in the pine woods is a familiar bird to whom the poet-shaman gives voice. Its call is both its own and, according to Buddhist literary and religious tradition, an invitation to the noumenal world.

What the shaman was to primitive culture, the poet and other artists are to contemporary re-inhabited space. Beyond the ecological and economical benefits of re-inhabiting place and living according to a bioregional ethic, are spiritual benefits of place which poets voice. By re-inhabiting place through knowing the land and its lore, we can overcome alienation as people

> learn that community is of spiritual benefit and of health for everyone, that ongoing working relationships and shared concerns, music, poetry, and stories all evolve into the shared practice of a set of values, visions, and questions. That's what the spiritual path really is.
>
> ('Bioregional Ethic', RW, p. 141)

Snyder's most extended discussion of the function of poetry in re-inhabited places appears in 'Poetry, Community & Climax' (RW) which is a revision and extension of ideas originally in 'Poetry and the Primitive: Notes on Poetry as an Ecological Survival Technique' (EHH). In 'Poetry, Community & Climax,' he gives a recent history of public poetry in the United States from the 1950s when Allen Ginsberg and others began poetry readings which inspired countless more. Snyder argues that people who gather for readings create a community that is more than literary (for example, the counter-culture). Among the poets who read, Snyder identifies the 'home growers'. These poets

> live in a place with some intention of staying there – and begin to find their poetry playing a useful role in the daily life of the neighborhood. Poetry as a tool, a net or trap to catch and present; a sharp edge; a medicine, or the little awl that unties knots.
>
> ('Poetry, Community & Climax', RW, p. 167)

31

Most such poets remain unknown outside their communities, but they express an alternative culture to that manufactured by television and newspapers. This kind of decentralized culture 'is as important to our long-range ecological and social health', Snyder claims, 'as the decentralization of agriculture, production, energy, and government' ('Poetry, Community & Climax', RW, p. 169). Such poets and their poems speak 'to what is happening *here*. They shine a little ray of myth on things; memory turning to legend' ('Poetry, Community & Climax', RW, p. 168). Snyder delights in the 'pleasure in the eyes of the audience when a local tree, a local river or mountain, comes swirling forth as part of proto-epic or myth' ('Poetry, Community & Climax', RW, p. 168). Given his own commitment to poetry, to place, to *here*, it is not surprising that Snyder regards as equal honors having been invited to read at the United States Library of Congress and at the North San Juan Fire Hall in his own watershed community ('Poetry, Community & Climax', RW, p. 169).

It is, of course, not Snyder's intention to encourage parochialism. A re-inhabitation of place that demands an experiential and intellectual knowledge of local biological and geological circumstances and an awareness of the wisdom of peoples who have lived there before, is hardly in the service of a provincialism that promotes ignorance of the larger world or hatred of those who live in different ways. On the contrary, Snyder believes, cultural diversity is as important to international stability and health in cultural matters as in the natural world. Moreover, just as it is for Snyder necessary to absorb the primitive to create a meaningful modern culture but wrong to aspire simply to the primitive, so the re-inhabited place is prerequisite to eventual solidarity with people beyond one's own group and to knowing that one's own watershed is part of the larger ecology of the planet ('Poetry, Community & Climax', RW, pp. 172, 173). The poet in touch with the particular energies of place is in touch with the energies of all places. This view is caught in 'River in the Valley' which depicts Snyder and his young sons Gen and Kai spending a Sunday outdoors exploring California's Sacramento River Valley. When one of his sons asks, 'Where do rivers start?' Snyder answers:

in threads in hills, and gather down to here –
but the river
is all of it everywhere,
all flowing at once,
all one place.

(AxH, p. 8)

Expressing the universal-particular paradox, Snyder invites his readers to 'find your place on the planet, dig in, and take responsibility from there' ('Four Changes', TI, p. 101).

NOTES

1. 'Does Bioregionalism Need An Open Fire (Wildfire) (Control Burn)?' *Raise the Stakes, the Planet Drum Review*, no. 10 (Summer, 1984), 3; "What's Meant by 'Here'," *Turtle Island* (New York: New Directions Publishing Corporation, 1974), p. 112; hereafter cited as TI.
2. See note 1.
3. James M. Houston, 'The Concepts of "Place" and "Land" in the Judaeo-Christian Tradition', *Humanistic Geography: Prospects and Problems*, ed. David Ley and Marwyn Samuels (Chicago: Maaroufa Press, 1978), p. 226.
4. *Myths & Texts* (New York: Totem Press, 1960); *Earth House Hold* (New York: New Directions, 1969); *The Real Work: Interviews & Talks 1964-1979*, ed. Wm. Scott McLean (New York: New Directions, 1980); *Axe Handles* (San Francisco: North Point Press, 1983); Left *Out in the Rain, New Poems 1947-1985* (San Francisco: North Point Press, 1986). Hereafter cited as M&T, EHH, RW, AxH, LR.
5. *The Old Ways, Six Essays* (San Francisco: City Lights Books, 1977), p. 65. Hereafter cited as OW.
6. San Francisco: Sierra Club Books, 1985.
7. See especially, Howard T. Odum, *Environment, Power, and Society* (New York: John Wiley & Sons, Inc., 1971); Eugene Odum, *Ecology* (New York: Holt, Rinehart and Winston, 1963); Raymond Dasmann, *Environmental Conservation* (New York: John Wiley & Sons, Inc., 1959); Ramon Margalef, *Perspectives in Ecological Theory* (Chicago: University of Chicago Press, 1968), hereafter cited in the text as PET.
8. *He Who Hunted Birds in His Father's Village, The Dimensions of a Haida Myth* (Bolinas, California: Grey Fox Press, 1979).
9. *In Search of the Primitive: A Critique of Civilization* (New Brunswick, New Jersey: Transaction Books, 1974), quoted in EHH, p. 126.
10. 'Good, Wild, Sacred', *CoEvolution Quarterly*, no. 39 (Fall, 1983), p. 17.
11. *He Who Hunted Birds*, pp. 93-95.

Place in Recent Native American Fiction

Richard E. Fisher

> There is a place
> I have often seen,
> more real than this room
> or the pen in my hand.

Joseph Bruchac, 'Ktchi Wadzo' in *Long Memory and Other Poems*

> i am hunting down a lost path
>
> toward home

Lance Henson, 'consider the stars' in *this small sound*

Place: address; bearings; course; direction; heading; locale; location; locus; point; residence; site. And so on.

To approach my topic by using a generalization in the interests of convenience, contemporary Native American authors seem to feel that there are good Indians and bad Indians. The good ones find the place where (their creators say) they belong; the bad ones do not. The good ones opt 'Red', the bad ones opt 'White' – and are lost.

Putting it another way: *if* the mixture of bloods in your veins disorients you, listen to the [ab]original one. Or another way: *if* a clash of cultures causes you to wonder where you belong, listen to the old ways.

Native Americans are presumed to be 'native' – to be indigenous – to *some*body's notion of 'America' – but whose? and *where?*

I want to discuss one particular concept of place in contemporary Native American fiction: as the destination of a process that begins in *mirage* and moves through *possibility* to rest in *realization*.[1] The place I describe is, then, existential, located in both topography and psychology. This could be expressed as my attempt, as a reader, to calibrate the 'place' presaged in Joseph Bruchac's poem cited above (the reality of what is 'in the mind' is ubiquitous in this literature; if these writers are right, what Whites call 'psychology' is not a recent White invention!) – or to locate the 'home' known to exist if only you can find the lost path, as in Henson's poem (that path has been despoiled by any number of White mistakes, but it exists in Nature (and in your nature); if these writers are right, what Whites call 'ecology' has forever been connected with the Native American sense of place).

My choice of this particular problem (managing to locate where you belong) means that I cannot consider other aspects of place in this estimable body of literature – such as the writers' inspired ability to show the reader the breathtaking spaces of land and sky in which their characters feel most at home, the geography to which they learn they belong. Nor will I consider the details of specific surroundings that add the beguilement of regional particularity to so many of their works. I will reluctantly have to pass over the enchantment with which they handle nuances of color, of sound, of the rewards of observation – being aware of what is around you in the place you happen to be. I have yet to encounter a Native American writer who does not excel in these things.

My choice, like my opening generalization, is largely motivated by the constraints of space, and it in turn motivates the selection of a few characters: N. Scott Momaday's Abel, James Welch's anonymous narrator and Jim Loney, and Leslie Marmon Silko's Tayo. Louise Erdrich's Gerry Nanapush, Lipsha Morrissey and Henry Lamartine Jr. are of course also relevant here, along with other characters by other writers, but will be mentioned only in passing.[2]

Convenience dictates the coincidence that these are all male characters. The importance of place (in ways both including and different from the one on which I focus here) is, of course, also revealed in the stories of a number of female characters not considered here.

Abel: *It was beautiful all around*

In a very real sense, all Native Americans have been uprooted. Historically, their original hospitality and generosity having been abused and exploited by progressive waves of White predators, they were either separated from their lives, or forcibly relocated in space, or both. Individually, the survivors on steadily contracting reservations have been disoriented by unavoidable contact with White culture and institutions. This methodical erosion of Red culture over the centuries has uprooted and alienated nations and individuals, corrupting societies and culminating in self-hate. How in the world can a

Red man perceive that 'It was beautiful all around'? And where? In what place?

As mentioned in my introduction, the answers to these questions are very existential. Before Abel, or any other (at least literary) Indian, can gain this perception, much work has to be done. It is hard work, and many other characters in these works fail. The work involves finding one's place – discovering one's self and locating it in time and space.

Like thousands of Indian men, and some of his colleagues in the literature considered in this essay, Abel has left a reservation life and performed military service for the government of the United States. Almost completely disguised in the uniforms of 'American' servicemen, these men have enjoyed the illusion of being received, or relocated, if not quite equally, at least seriously, in the dominant White society. The performance of their duties has been recognized and appreciated. They have experienced White living conditions, wages, and women. But wars, and conscriptions, come to an end. As veterans, they are out of uniform, out of a job, out in the cold.[3]

At first, upon sobering up after his return from the Army, Abel feels the pleasures of his old place, 'and for a moment everything was all right with him' (p. 32). But this turns out to be a mirage. Within a week, he realizes that 'his return to the town had been a failure, for all his looking forward' (p. 57). Trying to speak to his beloved grandfather, 'he could not say the things he wanted; he had tried to pray, to sing, to enter into the old rhythm of the tongue, but he was no longer attuned to it'. Soon, he kills a (White) man who has tried to kill him.

Emerging from prison seven years later, Abel tries to find a place in Los Angeles. Like other displaced Indians from various tribes, he seeks community, if not communion, in the Los Angeles Holiness Pan-Indian Rescue Mission, run by the Rev. J.B.B. Tosamah, Pastor & Priest of the Sun. Despite his knowledge of Indians and Whites, Tosamah (who doesn't come from a reservation) is a cynic who exploits alcohol and peyote for the 'good' of his citified Red men.

Abel is befriended by another Indian, Ben Benally, who seems to have been able to make a workable adjustment. Benally finds Los Angeles a 'good place to live' compared to where Indians had come from. 'There's nothing there, you know', he says, 'just the land, and the land is empty and dead. Everything is here, everything you could ever want' (p. 164). About Abel, Benally says:

> He was unlucky. You could see that right away. You could see that he wasn't going to get along around here ... You know, you have to change. That's the only way you can live in a place like this. You have to forget about the way it was, how you grew

up and all. Sometimes it's hard, but you have to do it. Well, he didn't want to change, I guess, or he didn't know how. ... [H]e wasn't as lucky as the rest of us.

(p. 135)

For all his compromising and philosophizing, however, Benally recognizes the difficulties for the reservation Indian trying to fit in somewhere else. 'You have to get used to everything, you know; it's like starting out someplace where you've never been before, and you don't know where you're going or why. ... You think about getting out and going home. You want to think you belong someplace, I guess' (p. 144).

Beyond this recognition, Benally anticipates a different future. He sees that Abel is lucky to be unlucky, to stop searching for a workable adjustment. When Abel decides he does not belong in L.A., he leaves – to go home. And Benally says:

> I prayed. He was going home, and I wanted to pray. Look out for me, I said; look out each day and listen for me. And we were going together on horses to the hills. We were going to ride out in the first light to the hills. We were going to see how it was, and always was, how the sun came up with a little wind and the light ran out upon the land. ... We were going to sing about the way it always was. And it was going to be right and beautiful. ... And he was going home.

(p. 172)

Whether or not Benally makes this journey and joins Abel, the novel concludes with Abel at home, if mainly only physically. His is not a triumphal return; the town, the valley and his very soul lie locked in winter, and his grandfather is dying. '[Abel] had gone out on the first and second days and got drunk. He wanted to go out on the third, but he had no money and it was bitter cold and he was sick and in pain.' So for six days, he has been attending his grandfather, listening to his voice at dawn: 'He heard it now, but it had no meaning. The random words fell together and made no sense' (p. 175).

Yet, during this death watch, he continues to listen, albeit without hope. 'His mind was borne upon the dying words, but they carried him nowhere. His own sickness had settled into despair.' And something happens as he listens. 'The room enclosed him, as it always had, as if the small dark interior, in which this voice and other voices rose and remained forever at the walls, were all of infinity that he had ever known. It was the room in which he was born, in which his mother and brother died. *Just then, and for moments and hours and days, he had no memory of being outside it'* (pp. 175-6; emphasis added).

Attending his grandfather, Abel has little to do but listen, and in the process, become reconnected with what he has been told but only dimly remembered. 'The old man had spoken six times at dawn, and the voice of his memory was whole and clear and growing like the dawn' (p. 177). It might be somewhat clumsily speculated that his grandfather's dying in this way, in this room, enables Abel to heal, to be born again, to become re-located, to realize his return to this place. Before the first light breaks in advance of the seventh dawn, 'Abel was suddenly awake, wide awake and listening. ... Nothing had awakened him. There was no sound in the room. ... There was no wind outside, nor any sound' (p. 189). Awakened, then, by the old man's soul leaving his body, Abel 'got up and began to get ready ... he knew what had to be done'.

He prepares the body for burial, makes the funeral arrangements, and then participates in the ritual running – the race for good hunting and good harvests that begins with the dawn. 'He was running and there was no reason to run but the running itself and the land and the dawn appearing.' This running contains both ritual meaning and Abel's final (?) healing:

All of his being was concentrated in the sheer motion of running on, and he was past caring about the pain. Pure exhaustion laid hold of his mind, and he could see at last without having to think. He could see the canyon and the mountains and the sky. He could see the rain and the river and the fields beyond. He could see the dark hills at dawn. He was running, and under his breath he began to sing. There was no sound, and he had no voice; he had only the words of the song. *House made of pollen, house made of dawn. Qtsedaba.*

(p. 191)

Here, where the book ends, we have been prepared to understand its Pro-logue, where Abel is seen doing this running, and we are told that 'The land was still and strong. It was beautiful all around' (p. 7).

Anonymous: *[Mine] was the laughter of one who understands a moment in his life, or one who has been let in on the secret through luck and circumstance.*

James Welch's narrator in *Winter in the Blood* chooses not to reveal his name. (It is tempting to read this as a sign of his alienation, which is real enough at the outset. We must remember, however, that among some tribes, including the narrator's Blackfeet, there is reluctance to tell your name for fear it will bring bad luck.) He never does reveal his name, but by the end of the story, he has resolved the major ambiguity of his life: he has realized his identity, he has covered a great distance. He has understood something very important about 'distance'. He is able to tell one place from another, and to know where he is at last.

Admittedly, he has been lucky. He has discovered that his real maternal grandfather is not the pathetic half-White drifter, Doagie, but a true survivor of the old times, Yellow Calf, the hunter. This discovery makes him laugh: 'It was the laughter of one who understands a moment in his life, of one who has been let in on the secret through luck and circumstance' (p. 158).

Before he has that luck, makes that discovery, the narrator has known very hard times. The two people he's only really loved are dead – his father and his brother (in whose death he feels implicated, although obviously innocent). He shares this abandonment with Abel, who did not know who his father was and whose brother Vidal is dead. Similarly, Silko's Tayo in *Ceremony* has lost his cousin (and surrogate brother) Rocky (and he, too, feels implicated, although obviously innocent). Yet each of these three characters has an older man who is the bearer, the repository of not only love, but memory: more passively than actively, all three contain a fund of saving memory on which the younger protagonists can draw, when they are ready. (Tellingly, as we shall see, Jim Loney has no such fund on which to draw.) Abel has his grandfather, Francisco; Tayo has his uncle, Josiah; and this anonymous narrator discovers his real grandfather, Yellow Calf.

His mother (who attends the Catholic church of a priest who will not set foot on the reservation) wanted him to 'make it' in the White man's world. He tried, took his opportunity to work in the rehabilitation clinic in Tacoma, and he was much appreciated – or so he thought, until he discovered (via a racist nurse) that he was hired only as the 'token Indian' who would qualify the clinic for a federal grant. 'She turned out to be my benefactor. So I came home' (p. 22).

But, of course, he wasn't 'home' yet, any more than Abel was when he first returned to the reservation after his military service. He was in limbo, drifting between his mother's ranch on the reservation and the bars and fights in the off-reservation towns. No place made sense; a place for him to belong was truly a mirage. He was afflicted by an enormous problem of identity and belonging which he discusses in terms of *distance*. 'I felt no hatred, no love, no guilt, no conscience, nothing but a distance that had grown through the years.' After considering some possible explanations, he continues: 'But the distance I felt came not from country or from people; it came from within me. I was as distant from myself as a hawk from the moon' (p. 2). He is 32 years old and feels nothing for anyone; he belongs in neither Red nor White worlds – 'I was a stranger to both and both had beaten me' (p. 120).

There is another facet of distance, though, that he detects in Yellow Calf. Properly understood, distance can be used to locate self. How does this work?

Eventually, the narrator realizes that Yellow Calf has a distance 'that made it all right to study his face', which he had felt prevented from doing earlier. He studies the details of the face, and especially the blind eyes. 'But it was his eyes, narrow beneath the loose skin of his lids, deep behind his cheekbones, that made one realize the old man's distance was permanent. It was behind those misty white eyes that gave off no light that he lived, a world as clean as the rustling willows, the bark of a fox or the odour of musk during mating season' (p. 151).

Then he begins to understand why his father, First Raise, had come so often to see Yellow Calf. During these visits, perhaps, his father had found a way to narrow the distance between himself, in the present, and the past which should always be present, but which has been growing, well – distant (not least because of First Raise's involvement with alcohol and White employers). The narrator also discovers why Yellow Calf has remained where he is all these years: 'My people were here' (p. 153). This place makes sense: 'a world as clean ...'.

The place where Yellow Calf lives is only three miles from the narrator's home; not much of a distance, in terms of space. But now, having crossed that distance both physically and psychically, the narrator makes a connection with his feelings from boyhood, when his father first took him to visit Yellow Calf – without telling him why:

> Yet I had felt it then, that feeling of event. Perhaps it was the distance, those three new miles, that I felt, or perhaps I had felt something of that other distance; but the event of distance was as vivid to me as the cold canvas of First Raise's coat against my cheek. He must have known then what I had just discovered. Although he told me nothing of it up to the day he died, he had taken me that snowy day to see my grandfather.

> (pp. 161-2)

The culminating sign of the narrator's healing, of vanquishing his apathy and sense of alienation, comes at the end of the last chapter (before the 'Epilogue'). Having – with great reluctance, be it noted – accepted the Quixotic and doomed challenge of trying to rescue a certain cow from drowning in the mud ('I crouched and spent the next few minutes planning my new life' (p. 169)), he can lie back and contemplate what he has learned: 'Some people, I thought, will never know how pleasant it is to be distant in a clean rain, the driving rain of a summer storm. It's not like you'd expect, nothing like you'd expect' (p. 172).

Gradually, convincingly, thanks mainly to the visits to the blind seer Yellow Calf, but also to his growing ability to cope with distances, he is enabled to appreciate a clean rain in a clean world, to come to terms, and to come home.

Jim Loney: *Once in a while I look around and see things familiar and I think I will die here. It's my country then.*

In this instance, I find myself having to assert that a heroic character can commit suicide. In this paper, I must evade the challenge implied (with a nod in the direction of Hemingway's Robert Jordan), and urge my reader to contemplate what James Welch does with it since, after all, it is he who raises the issue in his novel.

Of all the characters considered here, Jim Loney is the most alone. He is the most thoroughly disconnected. Like Momaday's Abel, Silko's Tayo, Erdrich's Lipsha and Welch's earlier, anonymous narrator, he has been deprived of normal family and parenting. His mother, a Gros Ventre woman, disappeared forever when he was an infant; his White father abandons him after ten years, and when he returns twelve years later, has no recognition for his half-breed son until Loney forces a confrontation just before arranging his own death.

Unlike these other characters, however, Loney has no link with an Indian past, no sense of an Indian identity, no older male to help (even Lipsha makes the crucial, and saving, discovery of his father at the end of *Love Medicine*). For him, more than for any of the others, his place in the great scheme of things as a half-breed is untenable: 'It would be nice to think that one was one or the other, Indian or white. Whichever, it would be nicer than being a half-breed' (p. 4). Unlike his anonymous predecessor in the Welch canon, he is *not* lucky!

Loney's problem is not the surroundings of Harlem, Montana; his natural surroundings (with one important exception) simply mean nothing to him. Why not just leave? Find a better place? He has opportunities: his sister Kate, who has 'made it' into a job with the federal government in Washington, D.C., tries to get him to accompany her there and start a new life. His White girlfriend, Rhea, bored with being an English teacher, announces that she is moving to Seattle, Washington, and wants him to go with her to start a new life. For Loney, though, there is no convincing prospect of a new life, 'not on this earth' (p. 175).

He has no stories, no memories or ceremonies, no traditions to draw on. Unique among these protagonists, he feels no relationship to the land, with one important exception: the butte that crowns Mission Canyon in the Little Rockies near his home, and which is the most important 'place' in the novel. Unable to live as neither-Red-nor-White, Loney contrives his leaving of this meaningless life by choosing the time, the method and the place of his death. Finally, this place makes sense to him. He finds a mission, climbs to the top of the butte where he proffers himself for the rifle shot from an Indian policeman and, as he falls, dying, thinks 'This is what you wanted' (p. 179).

The actions leading up to his (triumphant) death are so tellingly uncharacteristic that they must be read as positive: he has entered the realm of possibility. Previously, he has had no volition; he has been unable to make decisions (to see any point in making decisions); his movement (or lack of it) has been more accidental than volitional. Yet gradually (thanks to accidentally killing his friend, and then suspecting it was no accident), he has perceived how to transcend his situation – the possibility of finding a place where 'everything was all right and it was like everything was beginning again ... but ... not on this earth' (p. 175).

His chosen point of departure is the butte above Mission Canyon: 'It's my country' (p. 107).

Tayo: *He had arrived at a convergence of patterns; he could see them clearly now.*

As *his* story (one of many in Silko's novel) begins, Tayo is 'home' from the Pacific Theater, but lost, despairing, and insomniac: 'He had not been able to sleep for a long time – for as long as all things had become tied together. ... He could get no rest as long as the memories were tangled with the present' (p. 6). He has been made sick by the 'White' circumstances of his present state, crying and vomiting by turns – and the Army doctors can only say that 'the cause of battle fatigue [is] a mystery' (p. 31). Battle fatigue is not really the way to consider Tayo's sickness, his dis-ease.

Things are tangled up – Christianity, European names, the English language, serving in the White man's Army, becoming lost, cursing the rain, confusion (is it he or Rocky who is dead?), guilt ('killing' the rain, and Rocky and Josiah, bringing disorder to his village) – and there is much unravelling to be done. 'And there would be no peace and the people would have no rest until the entanglement had been unwound to the source' (p. 69).

His military service has taken him to the most extremely alien place that appears in these books. The jungles, with their suffocating enclosures, constant rain, and bewildering shades of green, have led to the death of his beloved Rocky (cousin/'brother'). While he has not made the mistake of following orders to mow down inconvenient prisoners of war, he *has* made the mistake of cursing the rain. He blames himself for bringing on the drought which is punishing his home place: 'So he had prayed the rain away, and for the sixth year it was dry; the grass turned yellow and it did not grow. ... and he cried for all of them, and for what he had done' (p. 14).

A calamity indeed, trying to come 'home' after the war and finding that *you* are the cause of its suffering. Like Abel, Tayo is infected, and he needs to purge himself, and to do so, he must visit many places – in geography and in memory. (Again like Abel: he is no longer 'attuned'; like Welch's Anonymous, he is negatively 'distant'; but unlike Jim Loney, he retains shards of memory, he has a 'usable past'.) He must make no mistakes: the White contamination must be expunged with care, because it is full of fatal temptations.

So, many places are introduced, or revisited. One of them is described in these promising terms:

> The place felt good; he leaned his back against the wall until its surface pushed against his backbone solidly. He picked up a fragment of the fallen plaster and drew dusty white stripes across the backs of his hands, the way ceremonial dancers sometimes did, except they used white clay, and not old plaster. It was soothing to rub the dust over his hands; he rubbed it carefully across his light brown skin, the stark white gypsum dust making a spotted pattern. And then he knew why it was done by the dancers: it connected them with the earth
> He became aware of the place then, of where he was.
>
> (p. 104)

Tayo gradually sorts things out. Sorts himself out. With his own persistence, and with other help: not least, from memory and ceremony, but also from men, dead and alive, and women, young and old, and from his quest through spaces where he comes to belong. (With his pursuit of the stolen cattle, cf. Welch's narrator's [more reluctant!] commitment to saving the spinster cow.)

And finally, healed and home, he is capable of a humorous (!) meditation when he is told what finally became of the book's outstanding villain (a bad Indian): '"California," Tayo repeated softly, "that's a good place for him"' (p. 260).

NOTES

1. That's why the *ifs* in my third paragraph are important; I do not mean to be misread as saying that Native American writers are narrow-minded, racist evangelicals on the warpath. We are dealing with a selection of characters who share a particular problem of *place*, and watching them earn a well-deserved rest.
2. These characters appear in the following editions, page numbers to which, when cited, will be inserted in parentheses in my text. Abel, in *House Made of Dawn* by N. Scott Momaday (1966; Perennial Library Edition, 1977); Anonymous, in *Winter in the Blood* by James Welch (Harper & Row, 1977); Gerry, in *Love Medicine* by Louise Erdrich (1984; Bantam Books, 1985) and in her short story 'A Wedge of Shade' published in *The New Yorker*, 1989; Jim, in *The Death of Jim Loney* by James Welch (Harper & Row, 1979); Tayo, in *Ceremony* by Leslie Marmon Silko (1977; Penguin Books, 1986); Lipsha, in *Love Medicine* by Louise Erdrich and in her short story 'The Bingo Van' published in *The New Yorker*, 1990.
3. For a study of the process, rather than its destination, involved in re-establishing Indian identity, in 'coming in from the cold', see my essay 'Look Homeward, Red Man: The Rocky Road to Rehabilitation in the Works of Some Contemporary Native American Writers' in *Allt om böcker* (Sweden, 1991).

Toni Morrison: The Black Search for Place in America

Darlene E. Erickson

Here is the house. It is green and white. It has a red door. It is very pretty. Here is the family. Mother, Father, Dick, and Jane live in the green-and-white house. They are very happy. See Jane. She has a red dress. She wants to play. Who will play with Jane? Come play with Jane ... See Mother. Mother is very nice. Mother, will you play with Jane? Mother laughs. Laugh, Mother, laugh. See Father. He is big and strong. Father, will you play with Jane? Father is smiling. Smile, Father, smile ... Look, look. Here comes a friend. The friend will play with Jane. They will play a good game. Play, Jane, play.

Our house is old, cold, and green. At night a kerosene lamp lights one large room. The others are braced in darkness, peopled by roaches and mice. Adults do not talk to us – they give us directions ... When we catch colds, they shake their heads in disgust at our lack of consideration. When on a day after a trip to collect coal, I cough loudly, my mother frowns. "Great Jesus, get on in that bed. How many times do I have to tell you to wear something on your head. You must be the biggest fool in this town." Later I throw up and my mother says, "What did you puke on your bed-clothes for? ... Don't you have enough sense to hold your head out the bed?"

So begins Toni Morrison's first novel, *The Bluest Eye*.[1] And so begins Morrison's literary attempt to speak from the perspective of the black person in America. The place described in the second paragraph, the black home of the likes of Pecola Breedlove, Claudia and Frieda MacTeer of *The Bluest Eye*, has little in common with the mythical house and family described in the first excerpt taken from the *Dick and Jane Reader*, the elementary primer read by thousands, perhaps even millions of American public-school children in the thirties, forties, fifties, and sixties. The textbook was beautifully illustrated and featured an ideal American family, all of them clean, beautiful, blond, blue-eyed and white. Those who lived in other houses were given to understand that they were effectively outside the mainstream; many were eventually wracked with desire for 'the bluest eye', as was Pecola Breedlove who was driven to madness by her desire to look like, even to *be* Shirley Temple, the white child star who came to epitomize the perfect American child. There was no room for an 'ugly' black child with woolly hair in a world that seemed to value only white skin, blond curls, and the 'bluest eyes'. (It might well be noted here that black children were certainly not the only ones left out of the *Dick and Jane Reader*. Many of America's poor and minority children probably shared that sense of deprivation. However, white or light skin did offer *hope*, however slight, that attaining the ideal was possible.)

Pecola's story is the parody of the American schoolbook fairy tale. She is raped and impregnated by her father and rejected by her mother. Pecola's mother, Pauline, the almost stereotypical black maid, neglects her own family and her own pitiful storefront apartment, devoting herself to her white employers, whose clean, well-stocked house and pretty little daughter are the closest she can come to the white culture's ideals of beauty and love which she has absorbed from advertisements and movies. The white myth of the selfless black servant, so prolific in American novels and films of the mid-century, is given a new twist in the hands of a skillful black writer. One sees the cost of such servitude, something one has perhaps not thought to see before.

But to return to the subliminal message of the *Dick and Jane Reader*, it is precisely this dichotomy, this sense of *not belonging* in this place, of being *out of place*, that is the subject of Morrison's work. Among the saddest and most tragic chapters in American history are those that deal with the destruction and enslavement of entire peoples in the name of progress. The stories of the elimination and/or subjugation of both American Indian and black slave populations in the quest for material progress, what seemed at the time to be the manifest destiny of a superior race over 'inferior' ones, are among America's most closely guarded national guilts. For although the United States has traditionally liked to see herself as the 'melting pot' of the world, offering a bright future to those immigrants who were willing to work hard, two groups, the displaced native Americans and the black slaves captured in Africa and brought to the new land against their will to provide a cheap labor force for the booming colonies, have generally stood outside the mainstream of even the *myth* of upward mobility and of cultural acceptance.

The external reasons for the plight of the black in America are not Morrison's main concern. Instead it is the *internal* ramifications of what it is like to be a displaced, a homeless, a culture-less people that has become Morrison's *raison d'être*. And it is not Morrison's contention that black Americans are history's only displaced, homeless persons. As a matter of fact, she makes repeated efforts to connect the story of these lost people to the entire tradition of history's 'lost tribes'. However, those efforts at connecting the black experience to universality bow, in Morrison's work, before the *specificity* of what it meant, and what it means to be black in a white world, a world where blacks have been made to feel they don't belong, that they don't have a history, that they don't have a place. Morrison asks some difficult questions about the specifics of history. Exactly what happens when one people takes another people by force from their homeland, cuts off all communications with their past, denies them their language, their very names, their dignity – even their humanity? What happens when an entire culture assumes, at least at some level, that this people is less-than-human, destined for the service of another race?

Today in the United States it is fashionable to believe that the solution to what is seen as the 'black problem' in the country is integration, absorption, the incorporation of blacks into the white mainstream. But black writers like Toni Morrison don't see it that way. And Morrison may well be the finest spokesperson for the black experience writing today. Her message tends to sound an alarm for most American whites. And perhaps it should, because Morrison is suggesting that any easy answer to America's racial problems, particularly a white answer, simply will not work. As Morrison searches both African and American history from slavery to the present day, she looks for ways to help blacks develop their own *sense of place*, their own sense of family, their own mythology, their own reasons for belonging, their own antidotes for *homelessness*. But in doing so, she, and other black writers as well, notably Alex Haley and Alice Walker, uncover the realities of what slavery and placelessness *really* meant. At the same time Morrison chronicles many of the reasons for the hopelessness of a contemporary black population effectively shut out from the very history of the land in which they now live through no choice of their own.

In Morrison's 1987 novel, *Beloved*,[2] there is a poignant passage wherein Paul D, an escaped slave running across the United States from the Sweet Home plantation in Kentucky, imprisonment on chain gang in Alfred, Georgia, and various other places of bondage, realizes that 'in all those escapes he could not help being astonished by the beauty of this land that was not his'. (Incidentally, the Sweet Home plantation is *not* at first a stereotypical showcase of slavery's horrors. Its owners, the Garners, have only six slaves, five male and one female, Sethe, who is kept for breeding. And they have encouraged the female to 'marry' (read *mate with*) only one male, Halle, a young man who has been allowed to purchase his crippled mother's (Baby Suggs') freedom by working through years of Sabbaths. The Garner slaves are treated quite extraordinarily well, 'like men', although Morrison allows that their assigned names are Paul A, Paul D, Paul F, and

Sixo *Garner*. The teenaged Sethe has successfully bred three children and is pregnant with a fourth; she is 'good stock'. It pains her that she must leave her own children 'in the grass' at the slightest whim of her mistress, Lilian, but the Garners are nonetheless 'good' masters, at least by any measure she has known.) I am assuming that it is not difficult for most readers to pick up Morrison's sarcasm in calling the plantation 'Sweet Home'. Even when slaves were treated unusually well, theirs was scarcely a 'sweet home'; in fact, it was not *their* home at all, a theme to which Morrison returns frequently. And when the Garners grow ill and die, there is no protection from the 'schoolteacher' who comes to take over Sweet Home and 'put things right'. After the schoolteacher takes command, any positive memories of Sweet Home disappear quickly. Sethe remembers that Sweet Home 'never looked as terrible as it was. It made me wonder if hell was a pretty place too. Fire and brimstone ... hidden by lacy groves. Boys hanging from the most beautiful sycamores in the world'.

Part of my own fascination with the *places* described in Morrison's discourse is the fact that they are actual places, places I have known, cities I have visited, rivers I have crossed. Morrison was born in Lorrain, Ohio in 1931 and when she constructs the stories of her characters, she puts them in *real* places, frequently midwestern, particularly Ohio locations. When Sethe and her four children escape from the Sweet Home Plantation in Kentucky and cross the Ohio River in 1855, they move through Cincinnati and are served by the Underground Railroad. (The Underground Railroad, a coalition of black and white abolitionists, helped runaway slaves escape to safe territory.) A portion of the Underground Railroad once ran through central Ohio; one can still see 'safe-haven' houses, like the one called simply '124' in the novel *Beloved*, in many small Ohio towns and cities. When Paul D crosses the Licking River, he crosses a river once named by Indians, a waterway one can still cross in central Ohio. When Sethe is saved from hanging after murdering her own daughter (and attempting to murder her three other children to protect them from being reclaimed by the schoolteacher, her new owner under the Fugitive Slave Law), it is The Colored Ladies from Delaware, Ohio, who draw up a petition on her behalf. These connections to actual places create an immediacy of location in the novels. In the twenties, thirties, and forties, the black people of Morrison's novel, *Sula*,[3] live in a neighborhood called the Bottom in the valley town of Medallion, Ohio. In *Song of Solomon*,[4] Macon Dead and the remnants of his family are trying to carve out a place for themselves in the North, in Michigan. In the novel the local city government continues to overrule any grassroots attempts made by black residents to put names on their own places. Blacks counter by continuing to offer cynical names of their own, names painfully indicative of their position as outcasts in a white world, names like 'Not Doctor Street', and 'No Mercy Hospital'. The importance of *naming* and the power to name is made clear in Morrison's novels. When Paul D despairs of regaining his own manhood he asks, 'Is that where the manhood lay? In the naming done by a white man who was supposed to know? One step off that ground and they were trespassers among the human race'. At the first opportunity, blacks chose their own names, especially when it came to naming their own children; and they were not usually the names of the white men who had owned them.

Although I have made passing reference to Morrison's works, I want to take a moment to establish their chronology:

1970 *The Bluest Eye*
1974 *Sula*
1977 *Song of Solomon*
1981 *Tar Baby*[5]
1987 *Beloved*, which won the Pulitzer Prize in 1988

In the interest of economy, I will restrict my discussion hereafter to two novels, *Song of Solomon* and *Beloved*, because they deal with the theme of place in a very special sense.

Song of Solomon might be called a work of magical realism. Set in the early sixties, it is the story of Milkman, a young and spoiled black man who yearns to fly – to break away from established society and his own wealthy but disfunctional family to new realms of possibility. In *Song of Solomon*, Morrison is in many ways the direct opposite of another black writer, Richard Wright. Wright finds no sustaining values in the past of black people, whereas Morrison celebrates the dead. Blacks did not drop in from nowhere. They go back in a long line of succession. There was a place, a beginning, a source. One finds among one's own ancestors heroes, cads, wonders and disappointments. But there is always *something*, a connection.

After a long, picaresque journey from Michigan through Pennsylvania and Virginia, Milkman finds a series of *places* that connect with his family history and eventually test his character and his very soul. History becomes a choral symphony in which each voice from the past that his father, the successful Macon Dead, tried to forget, comes alive and contributes to Milkman's growing sense of himself as somebody with a people, someone from a proud line of ancestors. Milkman surveys the acres which his grandfather cleared single-handedly. He envisions his father working that land, working, as he said, 'right alongside my father, from the time I was four or five'. When the Reverend Cooper from Danville says to Milkman,

'I know your people!' something changes forever in the young man. He has a place; he has a people. Reverend Cooper's story is ultimately a tragic one. Milkman's grandfather had cleared a fine farm, so well, in fact, that white men soon wanted it, so they shot the black farmer in front of his own children. They shot him from the back, 'blew him five feet in the air', as he sat on his fence for five days, trying to protect his farm and his two children, a daughter, Pilate, and a son, Milkman's father. When Milkman asks if they ever caught the culprits and arrested them, the Reverend Cooper responds: 'Arrested for what? Killing a nigger? Where did you say you were from?'.

But to his delight, Milkman finds that everyone in Danville loved his grandfather, the tall, magnificent Macon Dead, the 'farmer they wanted to be, the clever irrigator, the peach-tree grower, ... the wild-turkey roaster, the man who could plow forty in no time flat and who sang like an angel when he did it. ... He had come out of nowhere ... with nothing but free papers, a Bible, and a pretty black- haired wife'. Milkman's search continues into his grandfather's origins until he finds *his place* in Montour County, Virginia and his grandfather's real name, Jake, and his grandmother's name, an Indian name, Singing Bird. Jake was one of twenty sons, a Son of Solomon, or Shalimar, one of the Flying African Children. An old story persists that 'some of those Africans they brought over as slaves could fly – and a lot of them did, they flew back to Africa'. Somewhere in Milkman's past was a connection, a place, a brush with his own African origins, and a mythological relationship to greatness ... black greatness, not greatness as defined by any white man's measure. And no gun could ever change that.

There is a strongly mythical quality to *Song of Solomon*. Milkman takes up the Jason Myth, going in quest of his own golden fleece (bags of gold) and leaving behind his own self-destructive Medea named Hagar. He even encounters a wonderful old black witch-midwife named Circe who, like Pauline in *The Bluest Eye*, maintains a white family's 'big House' – but in a frankly anti-Faulknerian mode. Circe says:

> They loved this place. Loved it. Brought pink veined marble from across the sea for it and hired men in Italy to do the chandelier that I had to climb a ladder and clean with white muslin every two months. They loved it. Stole for it, lied for it, killed for it. But I'm the one left. Me and the dogs. And I will never clean it again. Never. Nothing. Not a speck of dust, not a grain of dirt, will I move. Everything in this world they lived for will crumble and rot ... and I want to see it all go.
>
> (*Beloved*, p. 45)

Intermingled with the Greek names and myths are biblical ones, with characters named First Corinthians, Pilate, Hagar, Magdalene, and, of course, Solomon ...

There is an enigmatic but joy-filled ending to *Song of Solomon*. Milkman *may* be shot by his own friend, Guitar, a young man caught up in the shadowy business of getting even with whitey. But death doesn't really matter anymore because Milkman finally finds Life, his own black Life. He finally becomes one of those very special Flying Africans. 'For now he knew what Shalimar knew: If you surrendered to the air you could *ride* it'. Morrison crystallizes her sense of the importance of black history when she writes: 'When you know your name you should hang onto it, for unless it is noted down and remembered, it will die with you'.

In her most recent novel, *Beloved*, Morrison moves even further back in time to the largely unrecorded, unnoted days before the Emancipation Proclamation which ended slavery, at least in a legal sense. Morrison depended on historical research for *Beloved*, research gathered largely from plantation diaries, death bed 'confessions', photographs and court records, for her reconstruction of what it felt like to be a slave. The story of the fictional character, Sethe, was based on the true story of a runaway slave named Margaret Garner who tried to kill her own children rather than let them be taken back by their new owner. The fictional Sethe succeeded in killing one child, a two year old daughter she called *Beloved*. The infant, Denver, born during an escape across the Ohio river, survived, as did Sethe's two terrified sons, Howard and Buglar, who walked away one day never to be heard from again. 'I couldn't let all that go back to where it was', Sethe says. 'I couldn't let any of em live under schoolteacher. That was out. I took and put my babies where they'd be safe'. That kind of love terrified everyone – certainly the schoolteacher, who declared his former property mad, a total financial loss. Even Sethe's new black friends were terrified of that kind of love, murmuring that there had to have been some other way. Sethe tries to explain her 'thick love' relative to place – 'Maybe I couldn't love em proper in Kentucky because they weren't mine to love. But when I got *here* ... there wasn't nobody in the world I couldn't love if I wanted to'.

The escapee Paul D worried about that kind of love. 'Risky, thought Paul D, very risky. For a used-to-be slave woman to love anything that much was dangerous, especially if it was her children she had settled on to love. The best thing, he knew, was to *love just a little bit;* everything just a little bit, so when they broke its back, or shoved it in a croaker sack, well, maybe you'd have a little love left for the next one' (*Song of Solomon,* p. 229).

The story of Sethe and her unspeakable deed is set in a particular place – one that becomes the heart of the novel – 124 – a safe house that had once belonged to a white abolitionist family. Sethe's mother-in-law, Baby Suggs, freed by her son, Halle, had made the house a place of safety and community for other escaped and freed slaves. Baby Suggs, whose slave name was Jenny Whitlow, bore eight children by six different fathers. Slave owners couldn't afford to encourage marriage because that might in turn encourage a sense of family and continuity, undesirable qualities in a subservient and saleable population. One of the novel's most poignant scenes describes Baby Suggs *hearing* that her two girls, neither of whom had their adult teeth, were sold and gone and she had not even been able to wave good-bye. Sethe's murderous deed cost Baby Suggs dearly and it cost Sethe herself the only sense of neighborhood and belonging she had ever had: 'Twenty-eight days of having women friends, a mother-in-law, and all her children together'. She had been junkheaped again and she knew it.

During the frantic escape from Sweet Home, Sethe became separated from the other slaves and from Halle when, almost nine months pregnant, she was taken to the barn and brutalized by the schoolteacher's nephews. They beat her until she was so scarred she had 'a tree on her back'. But worst of all they stole her milk, the milk she needed for her Beloved. Sethe discovers much later that the slave escape attempt had been severely punished, with most of the slave 'boys' caught and beaten and the vibrant Sixo mutilated and killed. Whatever happened to Halle – who may have witnessed Sethe's brutalization – she never finds out. So in Sethe's mind, Sweet Home has taken on archetypal nightmare proportions.

Sethe has a great respect for place, especially for a place like Sweet Home. She worries that her children will not really comprehend the horror of a 'Sweet Home', but decides in a kind of primal terror that they must never go there. She says, 'Some things you forget. Other things you never do. *Places, places are still there.* If a house burns down, it's gone, but the place – the picture of it – stays, and not just in my rememory, but out there, in the world. What I remember is a picture floating around out there outside my head. I mean, even if I don't think it, even if I die, the picture of what I did, or knew, or saw is still out there. Right in the place where it happened'. Sethe would never let her children return to a place where men and women and children were moved around like checkers, where school-teachers taught their students to examine black people and list their human characteristics on the left, their animal ones on the right. Sethe adds to that the vestiges of what she calls a 'rememory' before Sweet Home, when as a young child she identified the hanged body of her mother because it was marked with a cross. Some things must never be forgotten.

But 124 itself also becomes a place of terror, for it is haunted by a familiar, the ghost of Sethe's beautiful murdered child, Beloved. Sethe isn't surprised: 'You know as well as I do that people who die bad don't stay in the ground'. (Some readers might want to make the ghost of Beloved into the creation of Sethe's imagination, but most black critics agree that Morrison is tapping here an age-old African belief about troubled spirits walking the earth and making it part of a black person's reality.) At first the ghost only turned over slop-jars, gave smacks on the behind, caused gusts of sour air. Sometimes there was a pool of red, undulating light. 'It's not evil, just sad', Sethe explains. But when the spirit ghost is turned out by Paul D, it returns as a twenty-year-old woman, the exact age Beloved would have been had she lived. So Sethe and her family have to live with the complexities of entertaining a flesh-and-blood ghost, a ghost who draws out all of Sethe's humanity as if it were mother's milk.

The younger child, Denver, now eighteen, struggles with her mother's relationship with the ghost-woman. Denver thought she understood the connection between her mother and Beloved: Sethe was trying to make up for the handsaw; Beloved was making her pay for it. Yet she knew Sethe's greatest fear was the same one Denver had in the beginning – that Beloved might leave. That before Sethe could make her understand what it meant – what it took to drag the teeth of that saw under the little chin; to feel the baby blood pump like oil on her hands; to hold her face so her head would stay on – Beloved might leave. That she wouldn't understand that anybody white could take your whole self for anything that came to mind. Not just work, kill, or maim you, but *dirty* you. 'Dirty you so bad you couldn't like yourself. Dirty you so bad you forgot who you were and couldn't think it up'.

Surprisingly, the novel ends with some degree of hope, for Sethe discovers that she *has not forgotten* who she is, that with Paul D's help she still *can* 'think it up', and that she discovers, like Milkman, that *she* is *her own best thing*.

What it seems to me Toni Morrison is doing in her novels is offering an antidote for the lack of history, the lack of place many blacks have felt in this country. Their sense of homelessness is explained; and it is made understandable. Many of the specifics about slavery are staggering to both white and black readers. But like the specifics of the Holocaust, some of the dreadful realities need to be passed down from generation to generation. It is necessary to recreate the kind of scenario that Paul D describes when he recalls that 'He had already seen his brother wave good-bye from the back of a dray, fried chicken in his pocket, tears in his eyes. Mother. Father. Didn't remember the one. Never saw the other. He was the youngest of three half-brothers (same mother – different fathers) sold to Garner and kept there, forbidden to leave the farm for twenty years. Once, in Maryland, he met four families of slaves who had all been together for a hundred years: great grands, grands, mothers, fathers, aunts, uncles, cousins, children. ... He watched them with awe and envy.' But in spite of his tragic past, Paul D is alive, and like Sethe and Milkman, he is *his own best thing*. Their stories – and perhaps hundreds like them – must be told so that there will be a sense of families, and places, and histories to note and remember.

Morrison begins *Beloved* with a passage from Paul's letter to the Romans:

I will call them my people,
which were not my people
and her beloved
which was not beloved.

Morrison is asking her readers, black and white, to do the same, to name them 'my people' and to identify black history as part of the full history of the United States, no matter how terrible some of the details of that history might be. There is no longer a place for the mythical house of the *Dick and Jane Reader*. In this real kingdom, there are many mansions, and all of them deserve recognition as places that help Americans define who they are, as a totality of peoples, not merely as the generality of one race.

NOTES

1. Toni Morrison, *The Bluest Eye* (New York: Washington Square Press, 1970).
2. Toni Morrison, *Beloved* (New York: New American Library, 1987).
3. Toni Morrison, *Sula* (New York: New American Library, 1973).
4. Toni Morrison, *Song of Solomon* (New York: New American Library, 1977).
5. Toni Morrison, *Tar Baby* (New York: New American Library, 1981).

ACKNOWLEDGEMENT

I wish to express thanks for both the conversations and the suggestions provided by Bell Hook of Oberlin College and Valerie Lee of Denison University in the preparation of this paper.

Spatial Metaphors in Anne Hébert's *Les enfants du sabbat:* Within and Beyond the Confines of the Convent, the Cabin, and the Quotidian

Ellen W. Munley

The powerful spirit of place generated in the works of Anne Hébert forms much like a coral reef, richly layered from lived experience accruing through the centuries, incorporating disparate and far-away stories about who we are. Confinement and liberation, open and closed spaces, and the freedom to be one's self versus conformity to socially accepted roles characterize her novels. They name places hostile to life and favorable to psychological, emotional, or actual death in their titles: *Les chambres de bois* (*The Silent Rooms*), *Kamouraska*, *Les fous de Bassan* (*In the Shadow of the Wind*), *Le premier jardin* (*The First Garden*). But it is in *Les enfants du sabbat* (*Children of the Black Sabbath*), one of two novels which does not mention place in its title, that Hébert brilliantly illustrates the complex interaction among spatial, social, and cultural constructs in the life of an individual woman. *Children of the Black Sabbath* contains three clearly differentiated yet interlocking spheres, two of which alternately empower and disempower the central character, Sister Julia of the Trinity.

Sister Julia, née Julie Labrosse, belongs to the religious order of nuns known as the Sisters of the Precious Blood. In the novel's first sentence, we find the Catholic novice lying in her monastic cell, simultaneously transported to the mountain home of her childhood by means of a trance-like vision that recreates in vivid detail her parents' primitive cabin and its sensuous, natural surroundings. In this previous time and space, here integrated into the novel's present, she was a witch. From the very beginning then, the sister-sorceress incarnates an ambiguous figure whose symbolic representatives Hébert will expose in all their affinities and oppositions to demonstrate how little they resemble the woman of flesh and blood they overwhelm. After Sister Julia gives birth toward the novel's end to a creature whom the Mother Superior and the chaplain consider to be the son of Satan, she shouts a defiant warning to those entering her cell: 'I am the one who is the sister of the blood that is most precious!'[1] These words of caution underscore the disparity between the symbolic and the real, and the corresponding devaluation of the latter in the lives of women. Exploiting the comic and horrific elements inherent in introducing a symbol of eternal revolt into a stultifying world of conformity, the author offers us the bride of Satan in nun's clothing. Sister Julia relives the emotionally complex moments of little Julie's seemingly unfettered life while immobilized in the ampleness and rigidity of her religious habit.

The choice of a witch as the novel's protagonist places Hébert within a tradition of women writers in France and Québec which dates mainly from the 1970's when the sorceress began to function as both symbol and image to create a new female identity.[2] Among the most notable Québécois authors to incorporate the sorceress myth in their writings are Denise Boucher, Nicole Brossard, Madeleine Gagnon, and Anne Hébert. The sorceress serves as a device that at first illustrates the systematic inversion of the father's law as spelled out by prominent spokesmen such as Lacan. A more sophisticated use of the myth permits putting into question psychoanalytic interpretations of woman and all cultural associations relative to women that are charged with metaphysical and social values. In the first stage, utilization of the myth transposes good and evil and negative and positive valuations. The marginality of the sorceress permits her to escape stereotypical images of the virgin and mother. Woman as subject rejects her identity as object in valorising her difference and articulating her own truths. Her intimate connection with the body gives birth to writing that she (re)produces from within herself, leaving behind an already interpreted and 'recycled body'.[3] In the second stage of the exploitation of the sorceress myth, women writers try to avoid the false identities associated with women's roles. One of the identifications that mothers cannot easily escape, for example, is the devouring mother who is all-powerful, or the devoured mother who sacrifices herself to her family. A corresponding lesson offered by authors on both sides of the Atlantic is mistrust of simple reversals which leave binary oppositions intact and exclude the maternal and the feminine not yet lived or described by women.

Envisioning place as an influential factor in the creation of a personal history, *Children of the Black Sabbath* inextricably links a localized past to the sorceress-sister's attempts to describe her own experience and reconcile her past and present to her future. Sister Julia is the Sabbath's child whether as religious novice or as witch initiated to the cult of devil worship by her mother and father. A witch and reincarnation of the devil, her parents represent the inversion of Québec's established civil order and Catholic religion. Possessed by dark forces between the emprisoning walls of the convent and the rustic walls of the cabin that houses the Satanic rites on the mountain, Sister Julia seems destined for heaven or hell with little chance of forging an existence of her own choosing.

Before examining her chances and how they are rooted in the places of her past history, her present, and her future, let me briefly summarize her story. Julie Labrosse and her brother Joseph, children of Philomène and Adélard, grow up in a remote area designated as the mountain of B... . We might note in passing the rich associations and ironic inversion implicit in her parents' names. Philomena was a Roman martyr whose existence was so dubious that the Catholic Church suspended her status as a saint in 1961. Philomena in Latin also translates into Philomel, a figure in Greek mythology. Raped by her brother-in-law and saved by her sister, the two women are saved by the gods who transform them into a nightingale and a swallow to escape the brother-in-law's wrath. Adélard invites an association with the philosopher and theologian Abelard; Abelard and Héloïse were the famous 12th-Century lovers who married secretly and maintained a passionate correspondence after their separation and Héloïse's consequent entry into the convent. Adélard bears as much resemblance to Abelard as Philomène does to the innocent Philomel. Adélard impregnates his daughter with diabolical attributes through physical rape and initiates her to the world of shadows. She is consecrated as a witch and her mother's successor in the course of a black mass. The mother tries to initiate her son to Satanism through incest but fails in her attempt. Julie, who is in love with her brother, also fails to seduce him. In order to flee his milieu and regain a sense of innocence, Joseph becomes a fervent Catholic and joins the army. Before leaving for Europe to fight in the Second World War, he enters into a pact of fidelity with his sister whereby she enters a convent to escape the past and please her brother. When Joseph marries an Englishwoman, Julie feels betrayed and drawn again by the pull of her past, especially in view of the false innocence and hypocrisy that surrounds her in the convent. She turns the accepted order of the convent upside down and casts a death spell on her brother, his wife, and their unborn child. Depending upon which line of interpretation the reader follows, Sister Julia subsequently gives birth to a monster, the devil, or an ordinary child. At the novel's end, she either (1) lies triply imprisoned in her delusions, the convent, and an anesthetic stupor following childbirth; (2) takes flight into the night sky; or (3) flees the convent to meet a tall man dressed in black awaiting her in the street.

The questions that confront the reader are why Hébert has written a novel of such profound ambiguity and whether one interpretation might be privileged over the others. A possible answer lies in Hébert's exploitation of the myth of the sorceress throughout history in the person of this young woman. The author has done something most unusual in following the text of the novel *per se* with a bibliography of works consulted on sorcery, black magic, wizards, and witches. These sources, dating from the Middle Ages to the Twentieth Century, support the thesis that the sorceress has incarnated everything from pure evil and demonic possession to a reaction against the repression of society and women by the Church. In creating three intertwined circles of time and space for Sister Julia of the Trinity, Anne Hébert casts a number of mystifying spells on her readers in order to open their eyes. Prisons of thought and of the spirit become temporally and spatially concretized as the reader perceives not only the walls which were previously imperceptible but possible escape routes and openings that might be enlarged.

Nowhere does imprisonment isolate and suppress an unsuspecting individual more inexorably and acutely than in *Children of the Black Sabbath*. The close confinement Sister Julia feels inside the convent walls strongly evokes and becomes confused with the childhood memories noted in the novel's first sentence: 'As long as the vision of the cabin lasted, Sister Julia of the Trinity, her arms folded across her chest, motionless in her cell and all the ampleness and rigidity of her religious habit, scrutinized the cabin as if she would have to account for it on Judgement Day'. These souvenirs take shape inside an abandoned cabin on the mountain of B..., the shutters nailed tight with planks in the form of an X. In the middle of the one-room dwelling sits an antiquated, oversized stove and a sleeping bag redolent of 'the mustiness of a warm stable and putrid algae ... anyone would come to the realization that here is a place of origin' (*Children*, p. 85). Will Julie succeed in resisting the determinism lurking in this description of her childhood or will she exchange one prison for another?

This question will best be answered by examining it in the context of the myths and realities surrounding the sorceress throughout history. Indeed we might also view *The Children of the Black Sabbath* as a text of origins. It incorporates the progressive stages of the valorisation of the sorceress myth beginning with a reversal of traditional values and ending with a demonstration that the reversal built in this novel operates on an original opposition between the good sister and the evil sorceress leaving us no exit from a claustrophobic place where 'freedom rots on its feet' (*Children*, p. 24). In other words, the sorceress rehabilitated by the first stage of feminist criticism is reborn from ashes impregnated with religious dogma and demonology.

Deifying the demon or, in this context, making a goddess of the sorceress allows no escape from two intersecting circles. To find possible escape routes from the physical and metaphysical prisons for women in Western culture and enjoy some degree of personal freedom in day-to-day life, it is necessary to follow the lead of Sister Julia and be 'everywhere at once' (*Children*, p. 179). This comprehensive view of the clash of cultural symbols permits an examination of the gods and demons that make up the cultural context of the West.

To date, all the literary critical articles on Anne Hébert and *Children of the Black Sabbath* interpret the novel as a work of revolt against religious and social repression or as a condemnation of evil. Both interpretations ignore a crucial third alternative for Sister Julia *of the Trinity*. Before venturing a hypothesis as to what this third alternative might be and what trinity might be invoked in the text, let me closely examine the oppositions that echo throughout the novel and prepare this third possiblity. As mentioned earlier the Sabbath of the title refers both to the day consecrated to God as well as to ceremonies conjuring the devil. Beginning with the title, then, the reader encounters a long list of ambiguous opposites where the kingdoms of heaven and hell mutually lend each other their characteristics in the person of Sister Julia and, by extension, in the Sisters of the Precious Blood. Does Sister Julia, for example, bear the marks of Christ's sufferings on the cross known as the stigmata during Holy Week (*Children*, p. 122), or is she displaying signs of a nocturnal visit in time and space to the mountain of B... (*Children*, p. 121)? Is the 'strange Passion' she relives that of Jesus, or Philomène burned alive in the cabin following the local deaths resulting from one of her abortions and the impure bootleg alcohol which she concocted? Will Sister Julia accept self-effacement as a victim and fill the role of the ideal religious woman conceived by her beloved brother so that he might return safely from the war? 'I will be the integral woman, the total victim, the guardian angel, the guiding sister. Knitting. Praying. Sacrificing myself for ten, for twenty' (*Children*, p. 154). Or will she regress to her childhood victimization as a witch? During her rites of initiation, Julie was 'consecrated and burned': 'Myself fire and feeding the fire, I make up the Eucharistic host of our strange communion' (*Children*, p. 69). Adélard and Philomène offer their daughter to be eaten and drunk during the black mass celebrated in their cabin. It is important to note in passing that a close reading of the novel neither definitively affirms nor denies any of these contradictory possibilities. On the contrary, it sustains all of them from first page to last.

The sister-sorceress seems to hold the power of life and death over others far and near. The transformation of Julie Labrosse into Sister Julia rests on the pact between brother and sister according to which Julie renounces the devil in exchange for her brother's fidelity. 'Joseph swears that there will never be anyone else in his heart, but that as a consequence I will have to pay during the whole war' (*Children*, p. 154). When her brother marries the Englishwoman, the sorceress sets the machinery of death in motion: Joseph's wife dies at the same time as their newborn child. Joseph's death will supposedly come to pass during the Battle of Cassino according to the sorceress's predictions. Given the fact that the Christ embraced by Sister Julia with a 'love of stupifying penance' (*Children*, p. 177) is inseparable from her newly converted brother, and given that the sole means of maintaining her childhood pact with the young man is to transform her incestuous desires into privations, the curse that the sister-sorceress pronounces betrays Joseph and Jesus at one and the same time: '*Maudit. Baptême. Verrat*' (*Children*, p. 91).

However, in denying her brother and the God into whom he had been assimilated, Julie again finds the father who raped her when she was a girl. 'The red-haired man lies down on top of me. He pretends that he is the devil. I think that he is my father. My father is the devil' (*Children*, p. 64). Her mother confirms the paternal identity of the devil in caring for her daughter after the incident. Torn between the anguish engendered by her brother's rejection and her father's transgression, Sister Julia is scarcely better off having broken her religious affiliations. Certain critics, notably Serge Thériault and Maurice Emond, have emphasized the interpenetration of the spaces of the cabin and the convent. Thériault gives a detailed account of the double transgression committed by Sister Julia in adoring her brother instead of God and in denying her childhood and her identity as a witch while professing the Catholic faith.[4] Emond also envisions her as a true witch reassuming her original nature at the end of the book.[5] But we must realize that this exchange leaves us locked in a closed universe composed of two overlapping circles whose common area designates a space within which good and evil overlap and become confused (Figure 1). Sister Julia is such a charismatic presence in the convent that the other sisters begin praying to her as they pass by the door of the room where Mother Marie-Clotilde has her under lock and key. 'If my skirt just brushes the panel of the door shutting her in, I'll no longer always be served last in the refectory' (*Children*, p. 124). In another passage, Sister Julia appears in an inverted litany: 'Sister Julia of the Trinity, daughter of rape and incest, hear us, hear our prayer' (*Children*, p. 68).

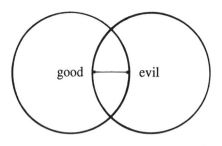

Figure 1

The reader can do no more than execute the steps of a dance of death in circling from one sphere to the other. The convent distinguishes itself as a mausoleum of the 'living dead' (*Children*, p. 175) when it does not resemble an asylum for the insane condemned to call nothing by its true name, to decide nothing, in effect to say nothing. 'To hope to attain, one day, absolute non-speech' (*Children*, p. 50) or, in other words, death. In the interval, the sisters must above all neither express themselves nor behave like adults. 'Blind obedience, innocent laughter, sweet foolishness, the frivolous sorrow of a scolded child ... the whole drowned in an incomparable silence. The bottom of the ocean rediscovered. Mother house. Mother womb' (*Children*, p. 50).

The revolt that Sister Julia declares in opposition to the death-affirming aspects of convent life in Québec during the 40's shatters the silence of the convent like the eruption of a hearty laugh. This death-defying revolt has been nourished since her childhood. Her parents offered ceremonies opposed to the interdictions of the clergy against dancing and alcoholic beverages. The poor of the area, otherwise totally submissive to the church and its exhortations in favor of the total obedience of wives to their husbands and of all parishioners to the parish priest, went to the mountain to tell or hear it told differently. 'Men and women ... called by their true names, never before pronounced, revealed at last in the silence of their blood. They came here to see life burst open' (*Children*, p. 107). It is therefore scarcely a surprise that in the aftermath of her rebellion, Sister Julia becomes 'the center of life and exists so strongly, among the living-dead, that it becomes intolerable' (*Children*, p. 175).

However, it is no less true that in several respects both adherence to demonic rites and practices and submission to the laws of the convent are linked to death. Water symbolism, for example, exists in both realms. In reference to the convent, Sister Julia conjectures that forgetting the little girl she was would mean that 'convent life would close in around me like the dead water of a stagnant pool' (*Children*, p. 32). On the other hand, Philomène communicates with her daughter through the medium of this same death pool: '... I can go back in time to the far-removed day when the waters covered the earth. My mother speaks to me through a pool. She tells me I possess a power and that I must exercise it' (*Children*, p. 149). In a penetrating article entitled 'Le retour des morts dans l'oeuvre d'Anne Hébert' ('The Return of the Dead in the Work of Anne Hébert'), Jean-Louis Backès notes the metaphoric link between the past and the world of the dead in her work. He further demonstrates how Hébert borrows from diverse sources to depict sorcery as drawing its life from the dead. Philomène takes possession of her own daughter: 'It's she! It's my mother. It's I. I am she and she is I. I am burning! It's my turn now' (*Children*, p. 161). Julie is condemned to relive death. During the course of the 'strange Passion' in the convent, she relives not only the series of cabins in the mountain of B... but all the excruciating details of the last days of the Labrosse family. We can only conclude that the life which bursts forth in Sister Julia is nourished to a far lesser degree by black magic than by a spirit of rebellion rooted in Philomène's and Adélard's rejection of the rigorous asceticism and social conventions prescribed by the Church.

Veering from one death to another, from the stifling aspects of religious life at its worst to a frighteningly credible world of evil and shadows nearly exhausts the forces of Sister Julia and of the reader who follows her incessant comings and goings between the mountain and the cabin. Fortunately, there is hope offered by a third reality to which the text refers from time to time. This third realm, which circumscribes the space where Julie finds herself at the end of the novel, is quite simply that of the commonplace, of everyday reality. For day-to-day living offers the only possible opening to a free zone in relation to the seemingly endless war between good and evil, between wide-ranging and conflicting definitions of the sacred and the sacrilegious. Waging this war in *Children of the Black Sabbath* entails the immolation of the sister-sorceress Julie who finds herself obliged to live this struggle in her body. She replaces Christ on the altar of the black mass or sacrifices herself out of love for her brother whose Catholic zeal denies the humanity Christ redeemed. Self-effacement in the name of love for Joseph includes not only physical mortifications but denial of herself and of everday life. 'I no longer have the energy, or even the desire, to cast a glance sideways, past my religious head-dress. No doubt God wants it this way, so that I might renounce the world in every image the city offers. I have only to pass through the world, like a blind person...' (*Children*, p. 16). At the beginning of the following chapter, we read: 'I ask just one thing of God:

to become a nun like the others for all eternity; to lose myself among the others and no longer show the slightest singularity.'

Several passages including the forementioned connect the action taking place between the forces of good and evil to life in the free zone. For Sister Julia's visits to the mountain as well as the physical signs of her Christian or Satanic possession might be interpreted as manifestations of a seriously aggravated nervous condition, depression, or psychosis. Delbert Russell favors an interpretation rooted in this world in his study of the book. In 'Saints and Demons: *Les enfants du sabbat*,' he envisions Sister Julia in a drugged sleep inside the convent at the novel's end, plunged even more deeply in her private hallucinations and delusions of grandeur by the anesthesia Doctor Painchaud administers after the birth of her baby.[6] Denis Bouchard, in '*Les enfants du sabbat* d'Anne Hébert: l'enveloppe des mythes', reduces the role of the supernatural and constructs an allegorical interpretation of the novel. He explains the juxtaposition of the cloister and the cabin, a sort of Rabelaisian convent in his view, as the process primarily responsible for the character of the novel: 'It is in this way that the work becomes an intermingled comedy, farce, and Medieval mystery'.[7] Although based on several aspects of the text, these two explications risk providing us with a captivating portrayal of the places past and present in Julie's life and give little attention to the last paragraph which opens onto the future. In other words, the cabin and the convent do not leave enough space for the quotidien full of possibilities.

The presence of three spheres of influence in the novel, as well as their equal importance in the text, is strongly supported by the tripartite configuration which structures the principal characters, time, space, and the narrative elements in *Children of the Black Sabbath*. The novel is, first of all, the story of Sister Julia *of the Trinity*. Her name does not allude to the Father, the Son, and the Holy Spirit of Catholic doctrine, but rather it ironically connotes the demoniacal family composed of the father-demon Adélard, the mother-sorceress Philomène, and their initiated daughter Julie. The latter is herself daughter, mother, and androgynous creator of the child to whom she gives birth before fleeing the convent. But does the novel sustain the supposition that Julie engenders her own child?

The realms of absolute good and absolute evil must be completed by the realm of the real where day-to-day life unfolds in order to enumerate the possible answers insinuated in the text. The problematic of the child's paternity, like all the other elements of the plot, has three replies. Let us continue, then, an articulation of the threefold construction of the narrative's key components in order to better understand the novel's structure and the open-endedness of the plot. Julie's identity encompasses Julie Labrosse, the sorceress eternally reborn as the daughter of Philomène and initiate to the Satanic cult; Sister Julia, the sister of the Precious Blood; an ordinary young woman. Philomène is the sorceress-mother, moon goddess; the sorceress-victim who unites herself to the sacrificial animal during the black mass and the failed sorceress who fails to seduce her son; a woman living in extreme poverty who sometimes works as a prostitute to earn money and is some-times beaten by her husband. Adélard's personage is comprised of the rein-carnated devil married to Philomène the sorceress; the devil-father-rapist of his daughter; a man who is out of work and living in abandoned cabins formerly used for the fabrication of maple syrup. Joseph is the childhood brother whom Julie desires; the combined Christ-infant Jesus figure whom Julie adores (*Children*, p. 153); the young married soldier who breaks the childhood pact of loyalty to his sister. The novel's time frame includes the 1930's in the cabin on the mountain of B..., the forties in the convent of the Sisters of the Precious Blood, and the future in the process of unfolding in the book's last paragraph. The space is that of the cabin, the convent, and the street outside the convent.

Who is the child's father? The space of the cabin identifies the demon as the father, or attributes to Julie alone and all-powerful the creation of the child. Another possibility bubbling in the witch's brew points to Joseph whom Sister Julia has appear in her cell and with whom she makes love (*Children*, pp. 149, 150, 155). Certain critics such as D. W. Russell propose Doctor Painchaud whom Sister Julia mysteriously summons and seduces. However, at the end of the novel 'a young man ... awaits Sister Julia, in the street' (*Children*, p. 187). What prevents the reader from attributing paternity to this young man or another? So much the more as Sister Julia, in order to escape in the next-to-last paragraph, uses the system of pulley, cords, and baskets installed in the transom of her cell by Mother Marie-Clotilde to communicate with the sister she has isolated from the rest of the community. '(This system) is *once again* a great help to her' (*Children*, p. 187). Justifi-cation can be found for all three hypotheses.

Julie's final disposition at the end of the novel likewise provokes extreme-ly varied critical interpretations. It is possible that the sorceress is flying high above in the night sky, a conclusion arrived at by critics such as Emond Maurice and Serge Thériault in their previously mentioned studies. Or, as Russell suggests, that Sister Julia is beyond reach, locked away in the convent and her self-delusional world. Doctor Painchaud's injection admin-istered after childbirth creates a dreamstate in which Sister Julia imagines the murder of her child by Mother Marie-Clotilde and the chaplain and her own escape through the window. A third possibility, set forth in this study, places Sister Julia in the street, no longer compelled to transgress either her childhood in the space of the convent or her religious vows in harkening back to the little girl who still inhabits her. In effect the last paragraph can be read to affirm any of these three resolutions. 'High above the sky is star-filled. The newly fallen snow gives off blue reflections. An extraordinary peace. The entire city is sleeping. A tall, thin young man, dressed in a long, black, tight-fitting coat, a felt hat drawn over his eyes, awaits Sister Julia in the street'. One might easily imagine the witch flying high in the night sky, looking down at the city and this young man who resembles other incarnations of the devil in the text, including Adélard and the husbands of Philomène's foremothers. Let me also note that the young man awaits *Sister* Julia. However, what emanates from these sentences is an extraordinary peace that emerges since, for the first time, Julie is neither imprisoned between the walls of the cloister nor spellbound in the magic space of the mountain. This peace that filters through the falling snow could only accompany liberation and resolution of conflict. It signifies that Julie has accomplished the goal she set for herself at the beginning of the novel, namely 'to free herself of her childhood cabin. Get rid of it once and for all' (*Children*, p. 7). She has relived all her childhood traumas and thereby gained insight as to who she is. Unable to either seduce her brother as a witch or to be the only woman of his life as a nun, Julie chooses to leave behind 'her cast-off religious habit of the Sisters of the Precious Blood' (*Children*, p. 187). The manner in which she dresses also symbolizes the end of the long line of sorceresses whose lineage ends with Philomène. Julie's mother always wore a pink dress and 'a blue straw hat trimmed with a flower and a bird ...' (*Children*, p. 28). Before descending into the street, Julie 'has put on the coarsely made skirt and jacket she cut from her gray flanelette blanket. On her shorn head, a white kerchief tied under her chin' (*Children*, p. 187).

Where then are we at the end of *Children of the Black Sabbath*? Like Julie, we are simultaneously within and beyond the three spheres of the cabin, the convent, and the quotidien. The sustained and profound ambiguity in the text rules out eliminating any one of these interlocking circles. Even in postulating Julie's freedom at the novel's close, we are reminded that the two other worlds of the mountain and the cloister do not disappear. They continue to coexist as strongly as the sister-sorceress Julia among her peers who renounce life. They concretize in the list of consulted works on the subject of sorceresses throughout the centuries that appears at the end of the book. The contradictory interpretations that we read in these historical sources provide us with a portrait of woman fragmented by philosophical, religious, and psychoanalytic thought. The spaces demarcated by the convent and the cabin serve as concrete metaphors for the social institutions and

traditional myths within which women often find themselves already interpreted and divorced from their own experiences. These prisons of thought
and society maintain order in the cultural context where, like Philomène's
followers, we end up devaluing women, 'adoring and cursing (them) by
turns' (*Children*, p. 109). Julie will never be able to entirely rid herself of
the attitudes of the saints and sinners who dwell on the mountain and inhabit the convent. She has, however, refused the roles of resplendent victim
as Philomène's successor and self-effacing victim as Joseph's tutelary sister.
She has succeeded in exorcising her own obsessions and in venturing forth
into the unknown territory of daily life.

NOTES

1. Anne Hébert, *Les enfants du sabbat* (Paris: Seuil, 1975) p. 184, hereafter referred
   to as *Children* in the text. All translations are my own and refer to the pages in
   the original French text. The novel was translated as *Children of the Black Sabbath*
   by Carol Dunlop-Hébert (Ontario: Musson Book Company, 1977).
2. Many of the Québécois writers contributed to a journal entitled *Sorcières*, published
   in France. This exploration of the figure of the sorceress among women writers,
   critics, and theoreticians on both sides of the Atlantic was not absent from the
   United States and England. In whatever country it occurred, authors played with
   language in an effort to expose hidden meanings and create new ones. One classic
   example in French revolves around the word *voler* which means to fly and to steal.
   Les voleuses de langue by Claudine Herrmann (Paris: Editions des femmes, 1976)
   exploits this word play in celebrating those women who have stolen language to
   free themselves from their traditionally silent role and taken flight through language
   by articulating their own experiences.
3. Nicole Brossard, *L'amèr ou le chapitre effrité* (Montréal: Quinze, 1977), p. 11.
4. Serge Thériault, *La quête d'équilibre dans l'oeuvre romanesque d'Anne Hébert*
   (Montréal: Asticou, 1980), p. 166.
5. Emond Maurice, *La femme à la fenêtre: l'univers symbolique d'Anne Hébert dans
   Les chambres de bois, Kamouraska et Les enfants du sabbat* (Québec: Presses de
   l'Université Laval, 1984), p. 323.
6. Delbert W. Russell, *Anne Hébert* (Boston: Twayne, 1983) pp. 102-103.
7. Denis Bouchard, 'Les enfants du sabbat d'Anne Hébert: l'enveloppe des mythes',
   Voix et images, Vol. 1, no. 3 (avril 1976), p. 381.

Strategies of Replacement: Raymond Federman's *To Whom It May Concern*

Joseph C. Schöpp

Raymond Federman's early works of fiction *Double or Nothing* (1971) and *Take It or Leave It* (1976), two typical literary products of the iconoclastic sixties and seventies, were deeply marked by the postmodern 'condition of placelessness'.[1] Their restless protagonists, aimlessly wandering from place to place, may be seen as the perfect cultural embodiments of the period. Always on the move, they breathe the spirit of a time which manifested itself most distinctly in such cult-books as Jack Kerouac's *On the Road* or Robert M. Pirsig's *Zen and the Art of Motorcycle Maintenance*, books which deliberately based their narratives on indefinite plans and whose protagonists liked 'more to travel than to arrive anywhere'.[2] They never bemoaned their placelessness as a loss, but in accordance with the dominant feeling of the time, they celebrated it as a truly liberating experience, since 'for the culture of the sixties the watchword was *liberation*'.[3] Wilfully violating the traditional narrative categories of time, place and character, Federman's early novels literally revelled in experimental game-playing and thus may rightly be regarded as true works of 'laughterature' rather than conventional literature.

The author's more recent books *The Twofold Vibration* (1982) and *Smiles on Washington Square* (1985) seem to be subject to a more conservative paradigm of writing typical of the nineteen-eighties. Gone are the obvious, at times too obvious formal innovations, the typographical eccentricities, the frequent digressions, the long self-reflexive narratological sequences. They employ the narrative experiment in a subtler, less demonstrative way; they are 'altogether more fluid and relaxed, less typographically oriented'. Here 'Federman unfolds a *narrative of possibilities*, rather than one of impossibilities and "cancellation" as before'.[4] What the reader witnesses is an increasing readiness on the part of the author to ground his narratives topographically, to remember places of his childhood which he, in his earlier writings, so anxiously tried to avoid. Though always looming beneath the textual surface, they were never really allowed to come to the fore. One place now becomes central to Federman's writing. Ever since he published *The Voice in the Closet* (1976), it is this closet-image which recurs in his writings, is if it were 'a phantasmic repository' full of narrative potentials.[5] Whereas the earlier works allowed only brief, fragmentary glimpses into that dark place of the Parisian apartment, where on July 16, 1942, 'known in France as *le jour de la Grande Rafle*',[6] a mother hid her only son in order to save him from deportation, in his latest novel *To Whom It May Concern*[7] he at last seems ready to re-enter this former place of hiding and speak about this hitherto unspeakable 'closet moment', his 'real birthdate, for that day [he] was given an excess of life'.[8] The claustrophobic tomb thus miraculously becomes a womb. With the deportation of his family one Federman died, while the other was born, who through his writing was to achieve the true vocation of his name and become a real *homme de plume*, a man of the pen, a Feder-man. Like Melville's Ishmael he survived in a coffin-like space so that some day he could tell the tale. But why *he*? Was it merely by accident or maybe due to a grand design that *he* survived? This overwhelming question torments all survivors of the traumatic and cataclysmic massacres of Auschwitz, Dresden, and Hiroshima, as recent studies impressively show.[9] Not surprisingly, the survivor-narrator of *To Whom It May Concern* is obsessed by the same vexing question, and his act of narration may be seen as an attempt 'in order to understand my mother's gesture when she hid me in that closet, and in order to decipher the darkness into which I was plunged that day'.[10] The closet, deeply inscribed in him, seems to contain covert energies which may be used creatively since, according to Bachelard, every place 'that has been experienced is not an empty box'.[11]

The narratological difficulties, however, faced by the writer, writing under postmodern conditions and marked by the 'unforgivable enormity' (p. 10) of the Holocaust, are truly enormous. The self-reflexive narrator of the book is well aware of them, when he remarks that 'the access to an event of the past is never unmediated, that it is always manipulated by false restitutions. But he also knew that one must resists such restitutions, even if it makes it impossible to reach the truth' (p. 183). The past, in order to become accessible, requires a medium. It is always and only through the medium (writing) that it may be recovered. Under postmodern conditions this act of mediation, however, has become problematic. It can no longer be viewed as an innocent activity by which something absent may be represented through language, as more conventional theories of writing would maintain. Writing is, as Federman remarks, always performed on top of other writings. That is to say, writing 'is not necessarily about something; it is writing on top of something'.[12] Writing about a place of one's past, therefore, is no longer a literal reconstitution of that place, but a literary 'restitution', a substitution, an *ersatz*. According to this theory, writing is no longer able to recover a place, but it always replaces/displaces it. *Qua* writing it is always 'false', a fiction, a lie, but (as the narrator in the opening paragraph of the novel is anxious to note) a lie which may nevertheless 'fall into place to shape a truth ignobly wrestled onto the surface of the paper' (p. 9).

This directly leads to another problematic with which the writer writing under post-Holocaust conditions is confronted. Writing about the 'enormity' of the historic event poses truly enormous problems. How 'to shape a truth' and make sense of something which is so utterly without meaning? How to revisit a place so atrocious and fearful? How to speak about something which is basically unutterable? Speaking, however, is a necessity lest we forget and silence gain a final 'victory over the fiasco of history' (p. 107). To remain silent, the narrator notes, means 'vegetating in the immense space of my days, not to mention the horrible holes of my sleepless nights' (p. 34). Thus the postmodern writer writing in the post-Holocaust era faces a real dilemma. He, on the one hand, 'feels obligated to tell and retell the sad story, lest we forget',[13] while, on the other, the impossibility of retelling becomes all too obvious. Words fail where the survivor, due to the enormity of the event, experiences nothing but a 'paralysis of the mind'.[14] The paradox seems insoluble, as one of the two protagonists of the novel, an artist-figure, must experience himself. As a survivor of the Holocaust he wants his artworks, violent and raw pieces of sculpture reflecting his very personal emotions which cannot be molded 'into neat forms' (p. 175), to serve as historic markers commemorating his own past. And yet, though anxious to keep the memory of this past alive in his work, he inadvertently conspires with those forces which cover up, efface and erase history. Some of his works are exhibited in a museum of modern art, a 'gigantic structure made of glass and steel, painted bright blue and green' and built 'on that very spot' where his aunt's house once stood. 'What a fabulous piece of erasure', the narrator comments:

> What a scandalous substitution! The immorality of history replaced by the playfulness of modern art. The old shabby building transformed into a comic book scenery, and all is well again so that the fable can go on in the hysteria of urban renewal. They call that face-lifting, but it's really an effacement.
>
> (p. 107)

Art by definition functions as an act of replacement. Unable to represent what is past, it is doomed to make substitutions of that past. *To Whom It May Concern* knows about this dilemma. Thus it continuously vacillates between exposure and cover-up, it constantly negotiates between the necessity and the impossibility of speaking about the unspeakable, of recapturing something which is marked by a fundamental absence and, therefore, can never be fully recovered through language.

To Whom It May Concern relates the story of Sarah and her cousin who were separated after the Great War and now, after thirty-five years, are supposed to meet again. He, living and working as a sculptor in an unnamed Western country, is on his way to a country in the East, where Sarah lives and works on a camp-farm. Stranded in mid-journey at the airport of the very city 'where the two cousins were born, and where an unforgivable enormity was committed during the war' (p. 10), he waits for the plane to take off:

> Unable to concentrate on the book he is reading, he lets his mind wander. What would he have become if he had gone with Sarah to the desert thirty-five years ago instead of seeking fame and fortune elsewhere? What would he be today? Just a farmer like her? Certainly not a sculptor, an artist clinging to a vanishing reputation. These are the questions he has asked himself over the years. He often tried to imagine Sarah's life. He has always been fascinated by the desert, has always thought of himself as a nomad. He even calls himself a nomad.
>
> (p. 88)

And while his nomadic mind wanders, hers wanders too, while she waits for his plane to arrive. It never does. The tale, as it were, is not allowed to reach its *telos*, its place of destination. What it presents to the reader instead is a series of fragmentary reminiscences of the traumatic moments in this city. Told 'without any mention of time and place', everything happens 'on a timeless vacant stage without scenery. No names of places. No decor. Nothing' (p. 104). The story as a piece of *arte povera*, a universal parable, in which nomadic figures as in a Beckettian fiction aimlessly move through an abstract, nameless territory. 'To name a place, in fiction', says Henry James, would mean 'to pretend in some degree to represent it'.[15] *To Whom It May Concern*, however, works against this 'imposture of realism' (p. 107). It never pretends to represent what is fundamentally absent.

The whole 'grim story' (p. 104), appropriately enough, is embedded in a grim context. It is Federman's winter's tale, consisting of a series of ten letters written in the darkest, most discomforting season of the year, between November 20 and March 21 (the first day of spring) and, as the title indicates, addressed to an unspecified person. A careful reading, however, seems to identify at least one of the addressees, to whom the letters may really concern, as the author himself, situated outside the text advising, criticizing and encouraging his narrator in his attempt to tell the tale of Sarah and her cousin. The author is, as it were, the letter-writer's *alter ego*. Thus the reader encounters a narrative configuration which he knows from Federman's previous works of fiction: The real author (whom we have to assume outside the text) at least twice removed, in order to make the reader aware that an act of writing is always an act of displacement, that it is always marked by absence and never by presence.

But despite its impotence to recapture a past and to recover what is always beyond the reach of writing, *To Whom It May Concern* also has its powerful moments. As an act of signification it attempts to ascribe significance and to inscribe meaning into a virtual void as the sculptor fills the 'empty space' with meaningful structures.[16] Without writing the past would be unwritten; it would remain a black hole, an empty page. Man without writing would resemble the two protagonists, deprived of their homes, their families, their memories, and 'hurled into the great void' (p. 64). With the parents' absence they have lost their own past; it is 'erased', 'brutally exed out ... destroyed' (p. 15). It is this traumatic moment of the family's erasure which helps explain Federman's obsession with placelessness. It explains the recurrent X-X-X-X, a deeply disturbing 'design of his and her family's total absence. Their absolute erasure' (p. 15). It also accounts for Federman's *horror vacui*, his compulsion to speak, to throw light into the darkness of the closet, to fill its void with voices and the empty pages staring at the writer with meaningful shapes and designs.

Thus Sarah and her cousin, dispersed and displaced, in order to (re)create themselves are bound to become shapers – each in his/her own way. He migrates westward and becomes a 'wild reckless and yet sensitive artist', a 'mad chiseler of wood, stone, and metal' (p. 15), always anxious to fill voids. 'His whole life he had been obsessed with absence, and now he had found a way to render that absence present' (p. 72). She wanders eastward and settles on a camp-farm which, she remarks, at first 'looked like a dead volcano. It was an empty place. We tried to make it full, but the desert is stubborn' (p. 178), as stubborn as the sculptor's stone and the writer's medium, and yet, at the same time, a tremendous challenge to extort a 'garden from the desert' (p. 179), a shape from a shapeless stone, meaning from an empty page. Federman's notion of the artist as nomad struggling with the desert may owe something to Edmond Jabès, an Arabic Jew living in Paris, who has an intimate knowledge of the desert and is 'perhaps the only Jewish writer who implicitly acknowledges in his work the impossibility of speech when dealing with the Holocaust and the concentration camps'.[17] What Richard Stamelman finds so characteristic of Jabès's writings, the white spaces between words, the margins that surround the writing, the open-ended quality of the discourse, the infinite *mise-en-abime* of questions (to which no answers other than more questions are given), the fragmentary quota-tions ..., the absence of narrative continuity, and the progression of self-displacing books circling around one another like an infinitely extensible spiral,

are also the hallmarks of Federman's *oeuvre*.[18] Sarah and her cousin (like Sarah and Yukel in Jabès's *The Book of Questions*) are intensely aware that, in order to fill their void, they have to become makers, that is *poets* in the Greek sense of the word. They realize that 'while he wrestled alone with his pieces of metal and stone, they had wrestled with the desert to carve out these fields, and he will understand that theirs was the greater struggle, and the greater success, even though Sarah will insist that they have failed' (p. 182). Both are aware that it is 'out of that wound', inflicted upon them on that summer day during the Great War, 'that you and I have shaped our lives' (p. 184). This is 'the symmetry' of their story (p. 166), the shape which gradually emerges and becomes increasingly significant as the book progresses. Groping in darkness during a long winter of discontent and discomfort, the novel eventually discovers its form when spring approaches. What at first looks like a mere rehearsal, a narrative try-out, as it were, in the final letter turns into a performance of sorts. The writer of the letters, 'no longer the director of the cousins' drama' and literally carried away by it, now becomes 'just one of its spectators' (p. 173). The story told con-sumes, as it were, its own teller. Projected onto a huge imaginary screen, he watches the cousins (his creations) embracing, hears them talking while he listens, 'their faces fading into darkness, their voices becoming more and more faint', until he finally realizes 'that their story would always remain unfinished' (p. 185). Though the artist continuously digs in 'to see where raw words and fundamental sounds are buried', though he feels compelled to tell about 'the great silence within' (p. 86), the telling itself is the most difficult and problematic part of the whole undertaking. It all too often ends in cheap and sentimental soap-opera passages, inoffensive and totally incon-gruous with the enormity of the subject. Thus Sarah's encounter with Josette, a Parisian prostitute protecting her from the Gestapo, inadvertently turns into a tear-jerking Zolaesque melodrama; 'once a prostitute walks into your book inevitably all kinds of sad familiar tales come bursting upon you' (p. 135). Thus the final scene of the cousins' reunion, projected onto the mental screen, reminds the reader of a grand Hollywoodian finale. It is the novel's intentional strategy to articulate and to disarticulate, to form and to deform, even to cancel and to annihilate itself at the very moment of its consumma-tion when it finally seems to have discovered its tone, its form, and its meaning. What the teller throughout his tale attempted to make has to be unmade at the end. 'THE MAKING & UNMAKING OF A BOOK' (p. 166), which was one of the novel's original titles, articulates this de-creative double strategy, which is perhaps the most appropriate way of dealing with the enormous subject. It is perhaps the only way to express adequately what it means to write under the influence of the Holocaust which defies all meaning.

Like Federman's previous novels, *To Whom It May Concern* thus once again turns out to be a pretext.[19] Its original intention to tell the tale of the two cousins' reunion remains unrealized. Stranded in mid-journey, the delay becomes a deferral in the sense that the journey is not completed, the *telos* of the tale not reached. All kinds of digressions intervene which, though obsessively circling around Sarah and her cousin, are not 'able to grasp their story' (p. 128). Waiting in his antechamber of departure, a transitory and 'parenthetical' place (p. 10), which becomes a perfect spatial symbol of his nomadic existence, the protagonist, like the Old Man in *The Twofold Vibration*, once more re-enacts the primary closet-scene trying 'to decipher in the blackness of that hole the meaning of his mother's gesture' (p. 141). Like the Old Man he projects himself both into the past and into the future, remembers and pre-members, weaves himself into all kinds of imaginary stories which have to be told and yet, at the same time, remain pre-texts in the sense of narrative rehearsals, while the final performance only takes place on an imaginary screen and cancels itself at the very moment of its completion. Even the grand finale of the book remains a pretext, a film-script awaiting its own cinematic realization. And the digressions which again and again show a tendency to turn into real(istic) stories, have to be de-realized whenever realism threatens to take command of the act of writing. The 'imposture of realism, that ugly beast that stands at bay ready to leap in the moment you begin scribbling your fiction' (p. 106), is a permanent threat to the narrator of this story. It is the totalizing, the holistic claim of the realistic mode which discredits the 'enormity' of the Holocaust as a literary subject. To treat the Holocaust adequately in literature, if this is not a contradiction in terms, requires counter-strategies to the realistic mode of narration. Not articulation but disarticulation, not representation but deferral, not the completed text but the unfinished pretext are the characteristics of a literature of the post-Holocaust. Thus it seems only logical that the sculptor (like the letter-writer and the extratextual Federman himself) produces art-works which correspond to these characteristics. The figures which the sculptor shapes 'seem either to be struggling to come out and become or else receding into a condition of non-being' (p. 16). Like the novel itself '[his] sculptures often reach into abstraction. They do not reflect reality but the crumbling of reality in the mind. His aim is not so much to comfort or celebrate as to confront and disturb. There is nothing elegant or delicate about his method. It is violent and irrational' (p. 92). His sculptures, by emerging and receding, reflect the making and the unmaking of the novel itself, a novel which to the very end remains a pretext, a text unrealized and thus perhaps the most adequate articulation of something which cannot fully be articulated.

NOTES

1. Leonard Lutwack, *The Role of Place in Literature* (Syracuse NY: Syracuse University Press, 1984), p. 216.
2. Robert M. Pirsig, *Zen and the Art of Motorcycle Maintenance* (New York: Bantam, 1975), p. 5.
3. Morris Dickstein, *Gates of Eden: American Culture in the Sixties* (New York: Basic Books, 1977), p. ix.
4. Marcel Cornis-Pop, 'Narrative (Dis)articulation and the *Voice in the Closet* Complex in Raymond Federman's Fictions', *Critique*, 29 (Winter 1988), p. 83.
5. J. Gerald Kennedy, 'Place, Self, and Writing', *Southern Review*, 26 (1990), p. 500.
6. Federman, 'A Version of My Life – The Early Years', *Contemporary Authors Autobiography Series*, vol. 8 (Detroit: Gale, 1989), p. 64.
7. Federman, *To Whom It May Concern* (Boulder, Co: Fiction Collective Two, 1990). All page references will be identified in parentheses after each citation.
8. Federman, 'A Version of My Life', p. 64.
9. Among others see Robert Jay Lifton, *Death in Life: Survivors of Hiroshima* (New York: Basic Books, 1982).
10. Federman, 'A Version of My Life', p. 65.
11. Gaston Bachelard, *The Poetics of Space* (Boston: Beacon, 1969), p. 47.
12. Zoltán Abádi-Nagy, 'An Interview with Raymond Federman', *Modern Fiction Studies*, 34 (1988), p. 158.
13. Federman, 'The Necessity and Impossibility of Being a Jewish Writer', *fiction international*, 15, i (1984), p. 92.
14. Robert Jay Lifton, 'Beyond Atrocity', *Saturday Review* (March 27, 1971), p. 24.
15. Henry James, *The Art of the Novel: Critical Prefaces*, ed. Richard P. Blackmur (New York: Scribner, 1962), p. 8.
16. Eudora Welty rightly observes that 'Sculpture exists out in empty space'. See her essay 'Place in Fiction', in *Critical Approaches to Fiction*, ed. Shiv. K. Kumar and Keith McKean (New York: McGraw Hill, 1968), p. 251.
17. Federman, 'Displaced Person: The Jew/The Wanderer/The Writer', *Denver Quarterly*, 19, i (1984), p. 92.
18. Richard Stamelman, 'Nomadic Writing: The Poetics of Exile', in Eric Gould ed., *The Sin of the Book: Edmond Jabès* (Lincoln: University of Nebraska Press, 1985), pp. 94f.

19. For a more detailed discussion of Federman's notion of pretext see my 'Multiple "Pretexts": Raymond Federmans zerrüttete Autobiographie', *Arbeiten aus Anglistik und Amerikanistik*, 6 (1981), pp. 41-55.

Defying Taboos:
The Sense of Place in
William Styron's *Sophie's Choice*

Regine Rosenthal

By the time William Styron published his novel *Sophie's Choice* in 1979 he was a well-established author. Born in Newport News, Virginia, in 1925 he had launched his literary career with *Lie Down in Darkness* in 1951. This first novel, which received excellent reviews and sold well, was deeply indebted to the tradition and history of the American South and to writers of that region, such as William Faulkner and Thomas Wolfe, and it firmly established Styron's name as a Southern writer. With the following works – the novella *The Long March* (1953) and the novel *Set this House on Fire* (1960) – Styron proved less successful. *Set this House on Fire* got a mixed reception in America as it was felt to be long, complex and challenging, but it was received extremely favorably in France. The 1967 novel *The Confessions of Nat Turner* was a turning point in Styron's literary career in so far as it not only met with a highly controversial reception but also was bitterly attacked by many people, especially blacks, for its supposed historic inaccuracy, racism, and for the fact that Styron as a white person had chosen the perspective of a black I-narrator. A collection of polemical essays, published under the title *William Styron's Nat Turner: Ten Black Writers Respond* (1968), attests to this dispute. Despite the controversy Styron won the Pulitzer Prize in 1968 for *Nat Turner* and the book proved a big financial success.

Apart from the play *In the Clap Shack*, first put on stage in 1972 at the Yale Repertory Theatre, Styron's next work of fiction to be published was *Sophie's Choice* in 1979, a novel that remained on the *New York Times* best-seller list for over forty weeks. In *Sophie's Choice*, as in *The Confessions of Nat Turner*, Styron again proved his courage by turning towards the very sensitive subject of Auschwitz which he very well knew might cause, if not done carefully, another bitter controversy. Works that have followed since are the collection of shorter pieces *This Quiet Dust and*

Other Writings (1982) and the most recent autobiographical account *Darkness Visible: A Memoir of Madness* (1990), an intense, honest, and moving portrayal of Styron's own devastating struggle with mental depression.

Sophie's Choice is a novel based on the life of Sophie Zawistowska, a Polish Catholic survivor of the Holocaust who for a petty crime was imprisoned in Auschwitz and – having miraculously survived – was brought via a Swedish DP-camp to Brooklyn. The sense of place looms large in the book and for Sophie, Auschwitz is both a real place remembered and a synonym for suffering, horror, evil, and unspeakable guilt. In order to make Auschwitz come to life as a place in the full range of its connotations and historical embeddedness and in order to avoid any renewed criticism of inaccuracy and taking too much freedom with historical facts, Styron prepared himself for the task with a good deal of thorough research. He read the autobiography of Höss, the commander of Auschwitz, and the collection of short stories, *This Way for the Gas, Ladies and Gentlemen*, by Tadeusz Borowski; he studied George Steiner, Elie Wiesel, Hannah Arendt, Simone Weil, and Richard L. Rubenstein. He read autobiographies by survivors but he perferred not speak to any of them. He made it a point, however, to go to Auschwitz and see the place. As he explained in an interview, he understood only later 'to what degree the trip had been necessary. How absolutely necessary it had been to my perception of history to have seen the place, those barbed wires, those fences, those barracks, all those things one cannot believe even when seeing them'. He found it 'a horrible visit, beyond anything believable'. Even days afterwards he was 'still in a state of complete emotional shock, as in a coma'.[1]

By choosing Auschwitz as the central, overwhelming place of the novel Styron had entered into the controversy over Auschwitz as a taboo place for literature. Of the three kinds of literary texts on the Holocaust, works of survivors, works of those who perished, and writings about the Holocaust by those who were not there, the last category certainly is the most dangerous and problematic one. For this reason, a group of critics, among them Elie Wiesel as the most outspoken arbiter, simply denies any right and possibility of transposing the Holocaust into fiction. The victims only have the authority to bear testimony; those who were not there cannot fathom the unspeakable. Wiesel postulates:

And now a few words about the literature of the Holocaust or about literary inspiration. There is no such thing, not with Auschwitz in the equation. 'The Holocaust as Literary Inspiration' is a contradiction in terms. As in everything else, Auschwitz negates all systems, destroys all doctrines. They cannot but impoverish the experience which lies beyond our reach ... A novel about Treblinka is either not a novel or not about Treblinka. A novel about Majdanek is about blasphemy. *Is* blasphemy ... How can one write a novel about the Holocaust?[2]

George Steiner in his essay 'Postscript' argues along the same lines when he claims: 'The best *now*, after so much has been set forth, is, perhaps, to be silent; not to add the trivia of literary, sociological debate, to the unspeakable'.[3]

But there are attitudes different from this among the critics who feel that silence on the Holocaust is an inappropriate means of dealing with it. Alvin H. Rosenfeld, for instance, in his book *A Double Dying: Reflections on Holocaust Literature*, holds that 'if it is blasphemy, then, to attempt to write about the Holocaust, and an injustice against the victims, how much greater the injustice and more terrible the blasphemy to remain silent'.[4] The Jewish American writer Cynthia Ozick holds a similar view. Though she has a great, abiding fear of 'making art out of the Holocaust, [of] mytho-poeticizing, making little stories out of a torrent of truth' and though she worries 'very much that this subject is corrupted by fiction',[5] she neverthe-less has taken the risk of transforming the Holocaust into fiction in her two stories 'The Shawl' (1980) and 'Rosa' (1983).

Styron, who lays claim to a more personal concern with the idea of geno-cide than most Gentiles do due to his Jewish wife and his half-Jewish children,[6] chooses an I-narrator in the novel who starts out with no knowl-edge of the Holocaust at all and no experience and who slowly learns by degrees as the story unfolds. This I-narrator Stingo, a young American writer from the South at the beginning of his career who is clearly based on many autobiographical facts of Styron's own life, lays claim to a literary tradition on the very first page when he says in an allusion to Moby Dick 'Call me Stingo'. But at the start of the novel he is, quite obviously, only beginning to take shape both as a writer and as an independent, fully-developed self. 'I wanted beyond hope or dreaming to be a writer, but ... for the first time in my life I was aware of the large hollowness I carried within me. It was true that I had traveled great distances for one so young, but my spirit had remained landlocked, unacquainted with love and all but a stranger to death'.[7]

Thus, the unfolding events of the novel depict in a way the initiation of the I-narrator into experience and suffering, a learning process shaped on the pattern of the *Bildungsroman*. For only after a number of painful, abortive attempts is Stingo finally initiated into the sexual fulfillment which he so painfully longed for all along. At the same time, with Sophie's gradual revelations about her past, a much more haunting process is going on which brings about Stingo's initiation into evil and the suffering of human existence. In 1947, in a Brooklyn boarding house, twenty-two year old Stingo, who aspires to become the James Joyce of the South (SC, p. 132), meets thirty-year-old Sophie, the Polish Gentile survivor of Auschwitz, and her lover Nathan, an American Jew from Brooklyn. Embedded in and induced by the mad events of the present, Sophie slowly reveals details about her unspeakable past that grow more haunting the deeper she digs into hidden and shunted-away memories she never wanted to recall any more. In this process of listening to Sophie, Stingo – along with the reader – learns more and more about a historical past that he had not been aware of before.

> On the first day of April, 1943, the day when Sophie, entering Auschwitz, fell into the 'slow hands of the living damnation' ... I had not heard of Auschwitz, nor of any concentration camp, nor of the mass destruction of the European Jews ... my ignorance of the anguish hovering like a noxious gray smog over places with names like Auschwitz, Treblinka, Bergen-Belsen was complete. But wasn't this true for most Americans, indeed most human beings who dwelt beyond the perimeter of the Nazi horror?
>
> (SC, pp. 263-264)

With this statement the I-narrator and the overwhelming part of the readership are given a common starting point. By taking – in his I-narrator – the position of those who were not there but who want to find out, Styron identifies with the readers who are in the same position as Stingo and at the same time he defends his reasons for writing the book. The narrator, who is looking back on that summer of intense friendship with Sophie and Nathan, decides to fill those names Buchenwald, Belsen, Dachau and Auschwitz – that are bound to remain 'stupid catchwords' (SC, p. 172) as long as they are not fully understood – with life by turning to a specific person and a specific fate that can better explain the human implications of the Holocaust than any statistics do.

> And surely, almost cosmic in its incomprehensibility as it may appear, the embodiment of evil which Auschwitz has become remains impenetrable only so long as we shrink from trying to penetrate it, however inadequately ... I have thought that it might be possible to make a stab at understanding Auschwitz by trying to understand Sophie, who to say the least was a cluster of contradictions. Although she was not Jewish, she had suffered as much as any Jew who had survived the same afflictions, and – as I think will be made plain - had in certain profound ways suffered more than most.
>
> (SC, pp. 265-266)

Styron approaches the problem of having to deal with an overwhelming, threatening sense of place in his novel by breaking the locale down into a number of different places and slowly building up toward a sense of inevitable doom, a sense of doom that Rosenfeld criticized as misappropriating Auschwitz for a new Southern Gothic novel (Rosenfeld, p. 165). The three places that loom large are, generally speaking, New York, the American South, and Poland, but all three of them are further differentiated into more specific settings that are represented in turn by the three main characters Nathan, Stingo and Sophie. Starting out in Manhattan with the alienated Southerner Stingo, the story then moves on to Jewish Brooklyn, where Stingo forms a very intense and troubled friendship with Nathan and Sophie. Thus the three basic elements of the novel – Southern Protestantism, Jewishness and Polish Catholicism – each manifested in both character and place – first meet in the rooming house in Brooklyn, where in the early summer of 1947 the action starts in the fictional present of the novel and slowly progresses towards its climactic ending in the fall. While there is a clearly symbolic connotation of spring as a promising beginning and fall as pointing towards a tragic death, Styron works with place as being even more fraught with symbolism and meaning.

Stingo rents a room in the 'Pink Palace' that in its hyperbolic description is a real place, yet creates the feeling of unreality in the I-narrator. Due to the overwhelming pinkness of the rooming house, Stingo feels as if he is in the MGM movie version of *The Wizard of Oz* (SC, p. 38). He feels trapped and subject to disquietude that is like a premonition of the horrible and unbelievable details he is going to witness repeatedly in the relationship between Nathan and Sophie in the present and will gradually learn about Sophie and her past. While living in this Jewish neighborhood in the North, the promising young writer Stingo writes his first novel about the American South that will launch his literary career. Place, as he realizes, is a 'most valuable component of a work of fiction' (SC, p. 131) and thus he explains to Nathan, 'I don't think it's any big deal for me to be writing about the South ... it's the place I know the best' (SC, p. 137). But there is more to Stingo's relation to the South. It is not only the place he knows best in terms of its geography and atmosphere, he is also an heir to its tradition and guilt. This theme of Southern guilt in connection with slavery and race is elaborated throughout the novel both in relation to Stingo and his family and in more general terms. It is clearly intended as a less forceful though powerful enough parallel to the problem of evil and guilt inherent in place that is later developed in much more detail in relation to Poland and to Sophie. Both the American South and Poland, as Styron sees them, thus have a burden in common that adds a deeper dimension to their external likeness.

Poland is a beautiful, heart-wrenching, soulsplit country which in many ways (I came to see through Sophie's eyes and memory that summer, and through my own eyes in later years) resembles or conjures up images of the American South – or at least the South of other, not-so-distant times. It is not alone that forlornly lovely, nostalgic landscape which creates the frequent likeness – the quagmiry but haunting monochrome of the Narew River swampland, for example, with its look and feel of a murky savanna on the Carolina coast ... but in the spirit of the nation, her indwellingly ravaged and melancholy heart, tormented into its shape like that of the Old South out of adversity, penury and defeat ... In Poland and the South the abiding presence of race has created at the same instant cruelty and compassion, bigotry and understanding, enmity and fellowship, exploitation and sacrifice, searing hatred and hopeless love.

(SC, pp. 301-302)

The guilt feeling Stingo expresses over the money that his family earned and he now lives on as a young writer due to the unjustified sale of the teenage slave Artiste, the pangs of conscience he still feels over having abandoned his mother one afternoon when she was mortally ill, his self-reproaches over having left Nathan and Sophie when they most needed him to avoid a major disaster, are paralleled on a much larger scale with the figure of Sophie, her irredeemable guilt and her life-long history of victimization.

In the beginning, Auschwitz is not a place Sophie can talk about. She only mentions it in passing and tries to avoid it as much as possible. But the more Nathan in his mad moments insists on the question of why it is that she is still alive while the other prisoners at Auschwitz have perished, the more she feels obsessed with talking about it, with getting rid of a sense of guilt that for her is so inseparably and inescapably connected with this place. In these moments Stingo takes on the role of a religious confessor on whom she can unburden herself.

In retrospect I can see that it doubtless would have been unbearable to the point of imperiling her mind had she kept certain things bottled up; this was especially true as the summer wore on, with its foul weather of brutal emotions, and as the situation between Sophie and Nathan neared collapse. Then, when she was the most vulnerable, her need to give voice to her agony and guilt was so urgent as to be like the beginning of a scream, and I was always ready and waiting to listen with my canine idolatry and inexhaustible ear.

(SC, p. 177)

But, as Stingo also finds out by and by, this hideous sense of guilt that gradually comes to the surface forces her to make reassessments of her past and even to tell outright lies. Having first been presented with the picture of a happy childhood and youth in beautiful Cracow with loving parents and husband and a wonderfully liberal-minded father who helped the Jews wherever he could, Stingo eventually finds out about the obsession with Anti-semitism on the part of the father who tyrannically dominated her childhood from early on and about her unloved husband who adored her father and despised his wife.

These lies, Stingo realizes, are 'a hopeless and crumbly line of defense between those she cared for ... and her smothering guilt' (SC, p. 289). She has to invent them in order to avoid facing the terrible reality of the past, and especially the knowledge that she had not only been a victim at Auschwitz, 'but both victim and accomplice, accessory ... to the mass slaughter, ... a fellow conspirator in crime' (SC, p. 266).[8]

The two places in Poland that are increasingly foregrounded in Sophie's recollections are Warsaw and Auschwitz. Warsaw figures as the city of doom where she lived during the later part of the war, was arrested and kept prisoner at 'the infamous Gestapo headquarters – that terrible ... simulacrum of Satan's antechamber' (SC, p. 446) and from where she was finally sent to Auschwitz. Auschwitz itself is never described from the inside but the disaster it spells for Sophie's life is captured in the scene of her arrival at the ramp, together with her two children and friends from the underground, and in various moments at the house of the camp's commander Rudolf Höss, where Sophie spent about ten days as a prisoner. The setting when Sophie arrived in Auschwitz is one of particular irony. Despite being faced with certain destruction she nevertheless could not help noticing that on the first of April, the day of her arrival, it was 'prematurely warm and greenly burgeoning with spring, ferns unfolding, ... the air sunshiny and clear'. (SC, p. 463) Or when Sophie finally decides to talk about the un-speakable incident that took place on her arrival and selection at the ramp she captures the irony of the place in the simple statement 'On the day I arrived at Auschwitz ... it was beautiful. The forsythia was in bloom' (SC, p. 567).

The glimpses the reader gets of Auschwitz as a place are provided in much more detail in Sophie's various scraps of recollection of the crucial day in Hoss's house on which she had planned to seduce him in order to save her son. There, Styron gives a description of Auschwitz that is still seen from a certain distance, not daring to enter the 'heart of darkness'.[9] The image the reluctant Sophie captures from the staircase window is that of a tableau; it is both visual and informed by smell, but there is no sound she can hear.

Invariably, lines of boxcars stood waiting there, dun-colored backdrop to blurred, confounding tableaux of cruelty, mayhem and madness ... Sometimes she sensed that there was no violence at all, and got only a terrible impression of order, throngs of people moving in shambling docile parade out of sight. The platform was too distant for sound; the music of the loony-bin prisoner band which greeted each arriving train, the shouts of the guards, the barking of the dogs - all these were mute, though upon occasion it was impossible not to hear the crack of a pistol shot. Thus the drama seemed to be enacted in a charitable vacuum, from which were excluded the wails of grief, cries of terror and other noises of that infernal initiation.

(SC, pp. 317-318)

To this soundless vision the dimension of smell is added when Sophie has reached the landing and looks out through a partly opened window: '... for the first time that day the sweet pestilential stench of flesh consumed by fire assailed her nostrils with the ripe bluntness of an abattoir, so violently taking command of her senses that her eyes went out of focus' (SC, p. 324).

The more we learn about Sophie's victimization and knowledge of evil in Auschwitz, the more is revealed about the parallel madness in her destructive relationship to Nathan. Styron points out in an interview on Nathan's role in the novel: 'I wanted him to be Sophie's destiny, her last executioner. The process of Sophie's destruction began at Auschwitz; Nathan completed it in Brooklyn' (Interview, p. 248). This parallel development in the disastrous significance of place both in Sophie's recollections of Auschwitz and of the present in Brooklyn comes to a climax in a scene that Sophie hesitates for a long time to recount. In its extremely fragmented narrative structure it is an indication of the process of disintegration taking place in Sophie's life. Stingo – and along with him the reader – finally learns about a weekend Sophie and Nathan have spent together in Connecticut a few months after Sophie's arrival in New York. It is a weekend deeply ingrained in Sophie's memory, but one she had refused to talk about before because it was then that she discovered Nathan's addiction to amphetamine and cocaine and its devastating consequences for their relationship. It is a weekend of violent sado-masochism culminating in a suicide pact that does not come off. The backdrop to all the aggression and madness enacted by Nathan is the New England Indian summer. 'The incredible radiance of the foliage afire' (SC, p. 413) is likened by Styron on the language level to what happens on the plot level. In this long disrupted chapter, descriptions like 'the blazing marvel of the New England foliage ... this amok flambeau unique in all nature' (SC, p. 387) and 'the inferno of leaves' (SC, p. 404) underline the parallel function of setting and plot. 'They drive north ... through bowers and overhanging clouds and raging storms of multichrome leaves in aerial frenzy – here belching color like blazing lava, there like exploding stars, all like nothing Sophie has ever seen or imagined' (SC, p. 410).

83

Another aspect in the novel that is strongly connected with place is the ever-present sense and sound of music. Sophie had been brought up on music by a mother who was a pianist, and she loves music almost as much as life (SC, p. 95). Thus Cracow, the place of her childhood, meant happiness as long as it was immersed in classical music, music by amongst others Mozart, Haydn, Bach, Purcell and Gluck. Music was something she only shared with her loving, gentle mother, while it shielded her from her dreaded father who was everything that music cannot be (SC, p. 473).

In the rooming house in Brooklyn it is music again that Sophie submerges herself in immediately after work in order to find serenity and a sense of inner solace that she badly needs to overcome the hurts of her past. In fact, it was music that saved her in her early days in Brooklyn when she almost gave up on life. When, after days of deep depression following a finger rape in the subway, she finally switched on the radio and quite by accident listened in on Mozart's Sinfonia concertante, a piece reminding her of her young days as a music student in Cracow, she was totally overwhelmed and she felt called back to life by an irresistible force. Likewise, music also plays a decisive role on that previously mentioned day of Sophie's intimate encounter with Höss. Whereas the music usually heard around Hoss's house was in the category of 'Schmalz', Tyrolean yodelers, or 'The Beer Barrel Polka', Sophie on that particular day was completely taken by surpise by a fleeting instant of music by Haydn which 'later reminded one of the most imperishable sensations she retained out of countless fragmented recollections of that place and time' (SC, p. 280). Thus, music at this very moment achieved a power that transcended place: 'chill after chill coursed through her flesh; for long seconds the fog and night of her existence, through which she had stumbled like a sleepwalker, evaporated as if melted by the burning sun' (SC, p. 282). And stepping to the window she saw 'the magical white horse again', the beautiful stallion Höss himself had so admired before, 'grazing now, the meadow, the sheep beyond, and further still, as if at the very edge of the world, the rim of the drab gray autumnal woods, transmuted by the music's incandescence into a towering frieze of withering but majestic foliage, implausibly beautiful, aglow with some immanent grace' (SC, p. 282). When the music suddenly stops the ecstatic moment is over. Only an infinite emptiness is left and her perception of place has changed with it. 'And I looked again to see the beauty of those woods when I heard this moment of Haydn. But the wind had made this sudden change, you know, and I could see the smoke from the ovens at Birkenau coming down over the fields and woods' (SC, pp. 283-284).

In some instances music is used to underline the irony of the situation. When Höss, for instance, informs Sophie that she cannot see her son after all and Sophie realizes that all her efforts have been in vain, the music played in the background is 'Das Land des Lächelns' by Höss's favorite composer Franz Lehár. Or in the most haunting, cataclysmic scene of the novel when Sophie arrives at the ramp with her two children Jan and Eva and is asked by the selecting officer to make a choice between the two, to decide which one should go to the gas chamber and which one should survive, the welcoming prisoner's band in the background is playing the Argentine tango 'La cumparsita'. Finally, when Sophie and Nathan eventually succeed in their suicide pact in Brooklyn they die to the sound of music – to the powerful, transcending music of Purcell, Haydn, Gluck and Mozart. But again there is irony involved in the choice of music. For at Sophie's and Nathan's funeral it is not the music Sophie and Nathan loved in life that is being played but the rather 'vulgar utterance', as Stingo calls it, of Gounod's highly sentimental 'Ave Maria' (SC, p. 619).

Apart from music which serves Sophie as a positive escape from reality, there are more desperate ways of forgetting the haunting qualities of experienced place, of fleeing from her pervasive sense of guilt. One possibility of retreat Sophie attempts to accomplish is suicide by drowning, by giving up on herself in the here and now. The other alternative she tries is numbing her awareness by alcohol. The moderate amount of wine she initially indulged in together with Nathan is eventually replaced by whiskey, whose consumption steadily increases the more Nathan torments her with his accusations. The stronger her sense of guilt, the more urgent her need to unburden herself, to overcome her repressions and self-consciousness by means of alcohol. In the final analysis, her drinking is another manifestation of her suicidal tendencies, of her wish to transcend memory and place by merging with death.

The third possibility of escape for Sophie is the ecstasy of sexual fulfillment, and thus the erotic element is strongly present in the novel. Sophie makes love in order to forget the pain, to forget the present, and the losses and the horror of the past. Sophie's lust, as Styron decribes it, is 'a plunge into carnal oblivion and a flight from memory and grief ... a frantic and orgiastic attempt to beat back death' (SC, p. 603).

At the end of the novel the I-narrator looks back on his reaction to the events by going through his diary. There he finds the entry by his earlier self: 'Someday I will understand Auschwitz' (SC, p. 623). Now, with the distance of time, he realizes that he should have written then: 'Someday I will write about Sophie's life and death, and thereby help demonstrate how absolute evil is never extinguished from the world. Auschwitz itself remains inexplicable' (SC, p. 623). And he goes on to explain that the only way to grasp the enormity of a place like Auschwitz was to focus on the particular, to deal with persons he had known. 'I did not weep for the six million Jews or the two million Poles or the one million Serbs or the five million Russians – I was unprepared to weep for all humanity – but I did weep for these others who in one way or another had become dear to me' (SC, p. 625).

Thus Auschwitz, as depicted by Styron, is both a specific place in history and a generalized place of doom, a manifestation of absolute evil. It is exactly this point that critics like Rosenfeld have bitterly attacked. Rosenfeld denounces *Sophie's Choice* as 'another prominent example of the tendency to universalize Auschwitz as a murderous thrust against "mankind"' (Rosenfeld, p. 159). Along with Berger, who accuses Styron of 'de-Judaizing the Holocaust',[10] he feels that Styron is avoiding the real issue by 'removing the Holocaust from its place within Jewish and Christian history and placing it within a generalized history of evil, for which no one in particular need be held accountable ... To generalize or universalize the victims of the Holocaust is not only to profane their memories but to exonerate their executioners' (Rosenfeld, pp. 159-160).

By the same token, Rosenfeld criticizes Styron's choice of Sophie, a Polish Catholic, as the representative victim of the camps. Styron, however, both in an interview and in the novel, carefully explains his reason for doing so. He argues that though 'the Jews suffered more than anyone else during the Holocaust period ... they are not the only ones to have suffered' (Interview, p. 249). To ignore the other victims, Styron holds, is to minimize the Nazi horror. Sophie is made a Christian to demonstrate the totalitarian dimension of the Holocaust, for as a Jew she would have been but one more victim (Interview, p. 248).

In the final analysis Rosenfeld dismisses *Sophie's Choice* as totally inadequate and merely 'exploiting atrocity'[11] for cheap effect. 'In relating his story of a Polish girl who stole a ham and forever after suffered sexual, moral, and psychological abuse, Styron has written not so much a novel of the Holocaust as an unwitting spoof of the same' (Rosenfeld, p. 165). Though other critics have also found *Sophie's Choice* 'flawed in a number of ways'[12] and have reproved Styron for 'trivializing the Holocaust' (Berger, pp. 32-33) or 'embarrassing' the reader with his language of 'different shades of Southern purple',[13] almost all of them have agreed that *Sophie's Choice* is a most ambitious and important work.[14] Philip W. Leon decidedly refutes the criticism that Sophie should be Jewish: 'To protest that Styron has no right as a novelist to create a non-Jewish character who suffers in a death camp is as hollow as saying only blacks can feel degradation and suffering from being owned'.[15] Larzer Ziff and Richard Pearce praise Styron for his achievement in writing about Auschwitz. While Pearce claims that

Styron does not desecrate the experience of the victims – a fear that Wiesel had voiced but 'leaves the Holocaust unimaginable and unutterable' (Pearce, p. 285) Ziff sees himself justified in the view that there is a need to speak about the Holocaust, to connect to the unimaginable on an emotional level.

> The description of the journey of the trainload of prisoners from Warsaw to Auschwitz cuts through every callus that has grown upon our consciousnesses after our many exposures to holocaust literature, and in such writing, far more than in the story of Sophie herself, Styron does, indeed, assert art's power and thus art's right to break in upon even sacred silence.[16]

Thus, with *Sophie's Choice*, Styron has achieved the most important objective of his work. He has written about Auschwitz and conjured up the sense of destruction, gloom, evil, and guilt connected to that place due to his strong sense of obligation as a writer. He feels that he can and must use literature – though it cannot change the world in a radical way – to penetrate deeply into human awareness. 'Millions of people can read, and I believe that a book can work on their consciences. As a writer I have no other goal' (Interview, p. 255).

NOTES

1. William Styron, 'Why I wrote Sophie's Choice', Interview with Michel Bradeau (1981). James L.W. West III, ed., *Conversations with William Styron* (Jackson & London: University Press of Mississippi, 1985), p. 253. Hereafter cited in the text as Interview.
2. Elie Wiesel, 'The Holocaust as Literary Inspiration'. *Dimensions of the Holocaust*, lectures at Northwestern University by Elie Wiesel, Lucy S. Dawdowicz, Dorothy Rabinowitz, Robert McAfee Brown (Evanston, Ill.: Northwestern University, 1977), p. 7.
3. Georg Steiner, 'Postscript'. *Language and Silence: Essays on Language, Literature, and the Inhuman* (New York: Atheneum, 1977), p. 163.
4. Alvin H. Rosenfeld, *A Double Dying: Reflections on Holocaust Literature* (Bloomington & London: Indiana University Press, 1980), p. 14. Hereafter cited in the text as Rosenfeld.
5. Cynthia Ozick in a telephone interview with Kim Heron. 'I Required a Dawning', *The New York Times Book Review*, Sept. 10, (1989), p. 39.
6. William Styron, 'The Message of Auschwitz'. Arthur D. Casciato and James L.W. West III, eds., *Critical Essays on William Styron* (Boston: G.K. Hall, 1982), p. 285.
7. William Styron, *Sophie's Choice* (Toronto, New York, London, Sydney: Bantam Books, 1983), p. 28. All further page references are to this edition and are cited in the text as SC.

8. In his essay 'The Gray Zone' Primo Levi, a survivor of Auschwitz himself, deals in some detail with the ambiguous and precarious role of the victim, with 'this mimesis, this identification or imitation, or exchange of roles between oppressor and victim'. Primo Levi, 'The Gray Zone'. *The Drowned and the Saved* (New York: Vintage International, 1989), p. 48.

9. Richard Pearce in his laudatory review observes that Styron takes the reader no closer to 'the heart of darkness' than did Conrad's Marlowe. Richard Pearce, 'Sophie's Choices', Robert K. Morris with Irving Malin, ed., *The Achievement of William Styron*, rev. ed. (Athens: University of Georgia Press, 1981), p. 285. Hereafter cited in the text as Pearce.

10. Alan L. Berger, *Crisis and Covenant: The Holocaust in American Jewish Fiction* (Albany: State University of New York Press, 1985), p. 33. Hereafter cited in the text as Berger.

11. This is the heading under which Rosenfeld discusses *Sophie's Choice*.

12. Robert Alter, 'Styron's Stingo'. Casciato and West, op. cit., p. 255.

13. G. A. M. Janssens, 'Styron's Case and *Sophie's Choice*'. Casciato and West, op. cit., p. 275.

14. John Gardner, 'A Novel of Evil'. Casciato and West, op. cit., p. 251. See also Richard L. Rubenstein, John K. Roth, *Approaches to Auschwitz: The Holocaust and its Legacy* (Atlanta. John Knox Press, 1987) pp. 279-283 under the general heading 'What can - and cannot - be said? Literary responses to the Holocaust', pp. 254-289.

15. Philip W. Leon, 'A Vast Dehumanization'. Casciato and West, op. cit., p. 265.

16. Larzer Ziff, 'Breaking Sacred Silences'. Casciato and West, op. cit., p. 244.

Flannery O'Connor's Displaced Persons

Karl-Heinz Westarp

Her eyes like blue-painted glass, seemed to contemplate for the first time the tremendous frontiers of her true country.

Flannery O'Connor

Displacement is more than ever an experience that a growing number of people go through. Religious, political, economic reasons have driven individuals, families and whole tribes into the diaspora of leaving their native roots and finding a new existence in a foreign environment. Identification with the place of origin, though often desirable, is no longer possible, and identification with the new place and its traditions is necessary, but not easy. More often than not this leads to a traumatic sense of displacement, of existential uprootedness.

One of the places where many ethnic groups have found a new home is North America, the continent earlier known as the land of unlimited possibilities. Large contingents of immigrants from different parts of the world have settled here, some integrating into their new environment, others trying to counterbalance their displacement by moving into ethnic neighborhoods. The resulting frictions between 'natives' and newcomers have been studied in scholarly treatises and represented in works of fiction. Among those are the works of two renowned writers of the American South, Flannery O'Connor (1925-1964) and Walker Percy (1916-1990). It is characteristic that they present 'displacement' with its physical and spiritual dimensions. Post-lapsarian man is essentially 'displaced' and 'alienated', constantly in search of his proper place and his true self. Sarah Gordon has convincingly pointed out the essential similarity between Walker Percy and Flannery O'Connor in their interest in depicting protagonists who experience themselves as alienated 'castaways' who are 'homesick'.[1] In her discussion of O'Connor's 'Poetics of Space' Christiane Beck characterises this space as follows: 'The most conspicuous characteristic of space in this work is its pervasive hostility invariably aimed at man. The human world is shown to be an essentially homeless place, a world where children are left motherless ... O'Connor's world is one where man is fated from his birth to live as the prey of hostile spatial powers'.[2]

In 1953/54 Flannery O'Connor wrote a short story entitled 'The Displaced Person' (first published in 1954), in which she dramatizes the meeting between a white farmer, a 'white-trash' family, a couple of black farm hands and a Polish immigrant family. The story is set in the strongly traditional American South, where the Polish family of the Guizacs arrive shortly after World War II. Mr. Guizac is the title figure of this three-part novelette, but characteristically for Flannery O'Connor the experience of displacement has much wider implications: it affects all layers in this small society, and it does not only affect them in the physical sense of the word.

The Polish immigrants carry with them the culture, habits, work ethics and religion of their home country; but otherwise they are dispossessed. Similarly, the recipient society has its social, cultural, religious and politico-economical heritage; and they are 'in possession', they are 'justified' in defending their own. The demands on both sides are tremendous.

This is what Flannery O'Connor saw and described on the surface level of 'The Displaced Person',[3] where all characters experience displacement. In the first part of the story Mrs. McIntyre, the owner of the farm, and the white-trash Shortleys are in possession of their territory, their 'place',[4] whereas the Polish refugees are seen as displaced intruders. However, at the end of this part the first crisis occurs, the Shortleys are discharged from the farm, displaced. In the second part the Guizacs are in power, Mr. Guizac has 'replaced' the Shortleys. But a new conflict arises when Mr. Guizac tries to bring over his cousin from Poland. Mrs. McIntyre cannot tolerate this violation of the rules of decorum. Part three presents the climax in which Mrs. McIntyre and the returned Mr. Shortley violently 'displace' Mr. Guizac. In turn they are displaced, as O'Connor points out in the last paragraph of the story.

Most of what we know about the Guizacs is colored by Mrs. Shortley's eyes, through which we see them. Upon their imminent arrival Mrs. Shortley stands there, the ominous 'giant wife of the countryside, come out at some sign of danger' (CS, p. 194). Before they show up Mrs. Shortley has changed the Polish family's name into the derogatory 'Gobblehooks' and imagined the newcomers as animals. When they arrive 'The first thing that struck her as peculiar was that they looked like other people. Every time she had seen them in her imagination, the image she had got was of the three bears, walking single file' (CS, p. 195).[5] As far as Mrs. Shortley is concerned, they should have stayed 'over there', 'in Europe where they had not advanced as in this country' (CS, p. 196), in a Europe which she remembers from a newsreel as a concentration camp and of which her husband only has World War I trench memories, in short a Europe 'mysterious and evil, the devil's experiment station' (CS, p. 205). She certainly thinks that the American people have done enough for those Europeans who are

> Always fighting amongst each other. Disputing. And then get us into it. Ain't they got us into it twict already and we ain't got no more sense than to go over there and settle it for them and then they come on back over here and snoop around.
>
> (CS, pp. 206-207)

> She thought there ought to be a law against them. There was no reason they couldn't stay over there and take the places of some of the people who had been killed in their wars and butcherings.
>
> (CS, p. 205)

Later also Mrs. McIntyre adduces defence mechanisms in saying, "'This is my place'" (CS, p. 224) and "'I don't find myself responsible for all the extra people in the world'" (CS, p. 226). She intends to tell Father Flynn, the priest who had brought the Guizacs to her farm, 'that *her* moral obligation was to her own people, to Mr. Shortley, who had fought in the world war for his country and not to Mr. Guizac who had merely arrived here to take advantage of whatever he could' (CS, p. 228).

There are obvious reasons for this kind of attitude: everybody is afraid of the otherness of the newcomers, the unknown territory from which they come. And the Guizacs do behave differently in their new surroundings, a way of behaving which was second nature to them in their own native environment. When Mrs. McIntyre holds out her hand for Mr. Guizac to greet her, he 'bobbed down from the waist and kissed it' (CS, p. 195). They speak a different language, which makes communication rather difficult, at times painfully impossible, or so it seems. This gives rise to Mrs. Shortley's vividly imagined

> war of words, to see the Polish words and the English words coming at each other, stalking forward, not sentences, just words, gabble gabble gabble, flung out high and shrill and stalking forward and then grappling with each other. She saw the Polish words, dirty and all-knowing and unreformed, flinging mud on the clean English words until everything was equally dirty. She saw them all piled up in a room, all the dead dirty words, theirs and hers too, piled up like the naked bodies in the newsreel.
>
> (CS, p. 209)

What affects the rest of the characters most is the fact that Mr. Guizac is 'Thrifty and energetic', that he is 'an expert mechanic, a carpenter, and a mason' (CS, p. 201). His work ethic upsets the existing equilibrium on the farm and therefore he is felt to be a threat to everybody. '"He's extra and he's upset the balance around here"', says Mrs. McIntyre (CS, p. 231).[6]

Mr. Guizac's behavior to the blacks also disturbs the existing order. He hands over the young farm hand Sulk to Mrs. McIntyre to be punished for his theft of a frying-size turkey, but leaves 'with a startled disappointed face' on hearing 'that all Negroes would steal' (CS, p. 202). Even worse, prompted by family ties and true empathic commiseration he trespasses the rules of racial segregation by suggesting that Sulk should marry his sixteen-year-old cousin from Poland. 'Mamma die, pappa die. She wait in camp. Three camp' (CS, p. 223). This is so unheard of that Mrs McIntyre for the first time is shaken, and with shocked wrath shouts, '"I cannot understand how a man who calls himself a Christian ... could bring a poor innocent girl over here and marry her to something like that"' (CS, p. 223).

Worst of all, the newcomers' Catholic background causes suspicion, fear and contempt. 'The Whore of Babylon' (CS, p. 209) looms large in the story, personified in the figure of the priest, 'a longlegged black-suited old man with a white hat on and a collar that he wore backwards' (CS, p. 195). Mr. Shortley sees him as the extended arm of the Pope in Rome and Mrs. Shortley blames him for all that is happening. 'Mrs. Shortley looked at the priest and was reminded that these people did not have an advanced religion. There was no telling what all they believed since none of the foolishness had been reformed out of it. ... They got the same religion as a thousand years ago. It could only be the devil responsible for that' (CS, pp. 197-198; 206).

All these factors contribute to the impression that the Guizacs are physically displaced people, and they are made aware of this by their hosts. They move into a shack which is furnished in the most Spartan way since 'they didn't have anything of their own, not a stick of furniture or a sheet or a dish, and everything had had to be scraped together out of things that Mrs. McIntyre couldn't use any more herself' (CS, p. 196); yet their hosts think 'how lucky they were to escape from over there and come to a place like this' (CS, p. 196).[7]

The fact that Mr. Guizac *has* to work to earn his living and that he has nowhere to go upsets the balance on the farm, so much so that all the others are affected by it. First the Shortleys leave when Mrs. Shortley realizes the threat of being fired because of Mr. Guizac. This displacement affects Mrs. Shortley so deeply that she dies of a heart attack in the car that carries them away from the farm. Later Mr. Shortley returns as a revenger, for he blames Mr. Guizac for his wife's sudden death. '"I figure the Pole killed her ... She seen through him from the first. She known he come from the devil'" (CS, p. 227). Therefore 'it would give him some satisfaction to see the Pole leave the place' (CS, p. 227), to see him displaced once again. He considers himself as an instrument of God's wrath: 'Revenge is mine, saith the Lord' (CS, p. 233).[8] Mr. Shortley succeeds in displacing Mr. Guizac by arranging his violent death, cleverly covered as a tractor accident, an accident the possibility of which Mrs. Shortley had foreseen much earlier in the story: 'If don't no terrible accident occur' (CS, p. 205). However, Flannery O'Connor makes it clear that Mrs. McIntyre, Mr. Shortley and the blacks, who all witness the accident, share the conspirator's guilt in Mr. Guizac's death. Mrs. McIntyre 'had felt her eyes and Mr. Shortley's eyes and the Negro's eyes come together in one look that froze them in collusion forever' (CS, p. 234).

Mr. Guizac's violent death, his final 'displacement', results in the physical displacement of the entire population of the farm: the same day 'Mr. Shortley left without notice to look for a new position and the Negro, Sulk, was taken with a sudden desire to see more of the world and set off for the southern part of the state. The old man Astor could not work without company' (CS, p. 235).

Even Mrs. McIntyre, who had held on to the farm for thirty years and struggled for its continued existence ever since she had inherited it from her first husband, is now displaced. 'She saw that the place would be too much for her now ... and retired to live on what she had, while she tried to save her declining health' (CS, p. 235).

At the end of the story we realize that physical displacement not only affects one group of people, the refugees or the officially displaced people, displacement affects also those who feel safely surrounded by their possessions. But physical displacement is not all, it is indicative of a much more comprehensive metaphysical displacement. At no point in the story is the reader left in doubt about the presence of a metaphysical dimension: angels and the devil are mentioned several times, and we recognize direct or inverted references to the Bible.

Mrs. Shortley has an apparently insurmountable physical presence: 'She stood on two tremendous legs, with the grand self-confidence of a mountain, and rose, up narrowing bulges of granite, to two icy blue points of light that pierced forward, surveying everything' (CS, p. 194). But her eyes are capable of extraordinary outer and inner visions, which are triggered by the presence of Mr. Guizac. First she recalls 'a newsreel she had seen once' (CS, p. 196) about the atrocities of Nazi concentration camps and which prompts her to an inversion of 'the golden rule' of doing to others as you would have them do toward you:[9] 'If they had come from where that kind of thing was done to them, who was to say they were not the kind that would also do it to others? The width and breadth of this question shook her' (CS, p. 196). Her second vision concerns the blacks. Mrs. Shortley indulges in thinking of herself as their protectress against Mrs. McIntyre, who hopes that the Guizacs' arrival will 'put the fear of the Lord into those shiftless niggers' (CS, p. 199). She is fond of seeing herself as the blacks' friend: 'I hate to see niggers mistreated and run out. I have a heap of pity for niggers and poor folks' (CS, p. 207). Yet while her unseeing eyes do not recognize the beauty of the peacock's tail she has an inner vision of the displaced people's effect upon the blacks: 'She was seeing the ten million billion of them pushing their way into new places over here and herself, a giant angel with wings as wide as a house, telling the Negroes that they would have to find another place' (CS, p. 200).[10] As a person, according to her husband gifted with 'omniscience', Mrs. Shortley's vision penetrates physical reality. When Mrs. McIntyre remarks enthusiastically about Mr. Guizac, '"That man is my salvation!"' then 'Mrs. Shortley looked straight ahead as if her vision penetrated the cane and hill and pierced through to the other side. "I would suspicion salvation got from the devil," she said in a slow detached way' (CS, p. 203). She does not allow Mrs. McIntyre to understand what she means by this, but O'Connor lets Mrs. Shortley share her thoughts with the reader:

> She had never given much thought to the devil for she felt that religion was essentially for those people who didn't have the brains to avoid evil without it. For people like herself, for people of gumption, it was a social occasion providing the opportunity to sing; but if she had ever given it much thought, she would have considered the devil the head of it and God the hanger-on.
>
> (CS, pp. 203-204)

Mrs. Shortley's most comprehensive vision is triggered by the presence of the priest, whom she regards as the root of all evil. This vision, which is reminiscent of Old and New Testament vocational visions, prompts her prophetic message: 'The children of wicked nations will be butchered' (CS, p. 210). What are we to make of Mrs. Shortley's visions? On the surface she is a person thus gifted, but her prophesies do not reveal the voice of a good spirit; the voice seems distorted by selfishness. Mrs. Shortley does not really care about the blacks, she has no understanding of the pain and the human tragedy behind the concentration camp newsreel, she only sees the priest and Mr. Guizac as 'come to destroy' (CS, p. 210). The arrival of the Guizacs changed her life: 'With the coming of these displaced people, she was obliged to give new thought to a good many things' (CS, p. 204). Though not religious, she starts praying, '"God save me ... from the stinking power of Satan!"' (CS, p. 209). She reads the Bible 'with a new attention' in an obvious attempt to seek justification for her negative vision of the displaced people. She feels a vocation to defend the existing order against all intruders from 'over there', she feels called to destroy the priest's influence, to destroy the Guizacs, to destroy 'the devil'. Just before Mrs. Shortley discovers that Mrs. McIntyre is going to fire her husband she reads the advertisement, 'I have been made regular by this marvellous discovery' (CS, p. 211). Yet, on hearing that they will be discharged she does not recognize that the advertisement has gained a very concrete meaning for her. She has been made regular, all her giant strength is gone to smithereens, and what is left of energy she invests in collecting her things and her family and leaving the farm before daybreak. She is blind with defeat and anger: 'there was a peculiar lack of light in her icy blue eyes. All the vision in them might have been turned around, looking inside her' (CS, p. 213). After the heart attack 'her fierce expression faded into a look of astonishment. ... One of her eyes drew near to the other and seemed to collapse quietly' (CS, pp. 213-214). Mrs. Shortley is not only displaced from the farm, she is displaced from life 'here'. As Flannery O'Connor formulates it: her family 'didn't know that she had had a great experience or ever been displaced in the world from all that belonged to her' (CS, p. 214). O'Connor's last comment on Mrs. Shortley's displacement, 'her eyes like blue-painted glass, seemed to contemplate for the first time the tremendous frontiers of her true country' (CS, p. 214) shows, I think, that Mrs. Shortley's physical displacement also has a metaphysical dimension. But what is Mrs. Shortley's true country? Is she allowed to 'see' her true country only after death? Was she at the moment of death, in which her body resembles the newsreel bodies, granted some kind of *visio beatifica*? Her eyes drawing near to each other could indicate that her vision *in extremis* is turned upon herself, that she is eternally fixed upon herself. O'Connor does not solve the question. The quality of her great experience is affected by the reading of the rest of the story.

Also Mr. Shortley's life changes through the meeting with Mr. Guizac. Before his wife's death a quiet man of few words, he returns after her death as a revenger, who speaks daggers to Mrs. McIntyre and the entire surrounding community: 'he was not going to wait with his mouth shut' (CS, p. 233). He is a different person, 'The change in his face seemed to have come from the inside; he looked like a man who had gone for a long time without water' (CS, p. 227). He finally succeeds in displacing Mr. Guizac once and for all, but he leaves as a man burdened with the guilt of murder. 'Mrs. McIntyre had changed since the Displaced Person had been working for her and Mrs. Shortley had observed the change very closely: she had begun to act like somebody who was getting rich secretly' (CS, pp. 207-

208). Mrs. McIntyre is described as 'the one around here who holds all the strings together' (CS, p. 217); for years she had struggled with 'shiftless niggers', with poor white trash. She had survived three husbands, although her first, the Judge, who had left her the impoverished farm, is still strongly present in his tombstone and in his many clichés which comment on the behavior of the people on the farm: 'One fellow's misery is the other fellow's gain' (CS, pp. 203, 208); 'The devil you know is better than the devil you don't' (CS, pp. 208, 217); 'We've seen them come and seen them go' (CS, p. 214). Thus O'Connor creates the impression that Mrs. McIntyre never actually won the upper hand over her first husband. But her strength is underlined by the fact that she divorced her other two husbands, one to be put into an asylum, the other intoxicated somewhere in Florida. Therefore Mrs. McIntyre is respected as a person: 'nobody had put anything over on her yet' (CS, p. 197). O'Connor describes her as 'a small black-hatted, black-smocked figure with an aging cherubic face, ... as if she were equal to anything' (CS, p. 224). Again it is Mr. Guizac who affects and finally shakes Mrs. McIntyre. Her changing attitude to the newcomer is indicative of this. Before he arrived she distanced herself from him by calling him 'Gobblehook'. In the period of her growing esteem for him she calls him Mr. Guizac, who saves 'her twenty dollars a month on repair bills alone' (CS, p. 210). She regards him as her 'salvation', as 'a kind of miracle that she had seen happen and that she talked about but that she still didn't believe' (CS, p. 219), and with satisfied affection she calls him 'the D.P.' (CS, p. 214). But on noticing that he intends to bring his cousin over 'she was shaken'; now she calls him 'monster' and ends up talking about him derogatorily as the 'Pole'. Mrs. McIntyre tries to struggle against him, but feels her heart beating 'as if some interior violence had already been done to her' (CS, p. 224). She tries to keep up defence mechanisms against his influence, but she feels weak. She pleads not guilty when the priest talks to her about her moral obligation to the Guizacs; nevertheless, she keeps putting off the date of their discharge from her place. But when Mr. Shortley denigrates Mr. Guizac even further, Mrs. McIntyre is so shaken that she felt 'she had a moral obligation to fire the Pole' (CS, p. 233). Clad like a hangman she turns up on the site of his imminent violent death, yet she feels unable to fire him, frozen by paralysis.

Her meeting with Mr. Guizac and her conniving in his violent death displaced her completely: 'She felt she was in some foreign country where the people bent over the body were natives, and she watched like a stranger' (CS, p. 235). Almost entirely disabled and isolated, Mrs. McIntyre lives through her private purgatory in that the only person who visits her is Father

Flynn, who came to 'sit by the side of her bed and explain the doctrines of the Church' (CS, p. 235).

This leaves us with the question: Who is this Mr. Guizac, who functions as a catalyst, who causes physical displacement as well as deeper insight in the people he encounters? Who is he, admired and hated, but finally rejected, as the 'abscess' his Polish name indicates?

As we have seen, the Shortleys regard him as an emissary of the devil; Mrs. McIntyre feels he is 'just one too many' (CS, p. 231), who upsets the balance. The priest defends Mr. Guizac by directly comparing his situation to the one God's 'Only Begotten Son, Jesus Christ Our Lord' (CS, p. 229) found himself in. Mrs. McIntyre's angry comment to this is revealing: 'as far as I am concerned, ... Christ was just another D.P.' (CS, p. 229). In this comparison I tend to see a key to an understanding of the deeper meaning of the story. The parallels between O'Connor's 'D.P.' and Jesus are obvious. He too was a displaced person, whom the pharisees regarded as a threat to their position, whom they had removed and killed. He also brought with him physical and metaphysical displacement. Mrs. McIntyre and the Shortleys had to give up their positions, their possessions, their 'place'. They experience this as being removed into a foreign country; yet it enables them to contemplate their 'true country'.

Flannery O'Connor succeeds in this story in a double way, I think. She addresses herself concretely to a social and political reality, the problem of refugees, of 'displaced' persons. In doing this, O'Connor also describes our postlapsarian human situation: we are all displaced, we are in the world but not from the world, our eyes are held, but must be open to glimpses of 'our true country'.

NOTES

1. Sarah Gordon, 'The News From Afar: A Note on Structure in O'Connor's Narratives', *The Flannery O'Connor Bulletin*, vol. 14 (1985), pp. 80-87.
2. Christiane Beck, 'Flannery O'Connor's Poetics of Space' in Karl-Heinz Westarp & Jan Nordby Gretlund, eds., *Realist of Distances* (Århus: Aarhus University Press, 1987), pp. 137-138.
3. Flannery O'Connor, *The Complete Stories* (New York: Farrar, Straus & Giroux, 1971), pp. 194-235. Abbreviated title: CS. References in the text are to this edition.
4. 'Place' occurs more than 60 times in the text alongside numerous references to 'country', 'there', and 'here'.

5. In spite of their human looks Mrs. Shortley later thinks of them 'like rats with typhoid fleas' (CS, p. 196), like the animal 'carcass on which the buzzard alights' (CS, p. 197), and Mr. Guizac jumps on the tractor 'like a monkey' (CS, p. 202).
6. In a similar way The Misfit in O'Connor's story 'A Good Man Is Hard to Find' (CS, pp. 117-133) throws 'everything off balance' (CS, p. 131).
7. Here as in many other lines of the story we discover O'Connor's trademark, her covered attack upon the self-indulgent pharisaism of the hosts.
8. The quotation is from *Deuteronomy* 32,35 and *Romans* 12,19.
9. The rule is found in the book of *Tobit* 4,16. See also *Matthew* 7,12 and *Luke* 6,31.
10. Later in the story her husband refers to Mrs. Shortley as 'God's own angel' (CS, p. 227).

A Neighborhood Voice:
Eudora Welty's Sense of Place

Jan Nordby Gretlund

In some of her stories Eudora Welty enumerates a virtual flow of highly poetic names to bring to life the splendid flora of her native state. She often uses the exotic sounding names of flowers, bushes, and trees to detail a setting and to specify the chosen location and time of year. In one passage from 'The Demonstrators' she mentions roses, perennials, crape-myrtles, redbuds, dogwoods, Chinese tallows, pomegranates, pear trees and a falling wall of Michaelmas daisies.[1] The object of these poetic passages is to prevent generalizations, and specific names create a truly vivid picture. The poetic prose always has that function in Welty's fiction, it is not invoked as a mere indulgence in the color of a scene. She describes a place in detail because she is writing about human beings, and to understand and define them it is essential to locate them through details of their world. 'Their meaning must always bear on and be defined by what they came out of', as Welty put it in an interview.[2] People are not the same, nor are the places where they live, and this matters in fiction, as Welty shows in her famous essay 'Place in Fiction' (1956).[3] In important respects we are products of our native place and its history; in this sense 'fiction depends for its life on place'. The specific place could be one of the many houses so carefully described in Welty's fiction, e.g. the Shellmound Mansion of *Delta Wedding*, the MacLain House of *The Golden Apples*, the Renfro-Beecham Farmhouse of *Losing Battles*, or the McKelva House of *The Optimist's Daughter*. The specific narrative value of these buildings is what they convey about the people who live in them, which is a good deal about their background and about the lives they live, as their houses reflect their ambitions and disappointments. A description of a house may be even more evocative than any direct statement about the people living there. The houses are probably indicative of the economic background of the characters, so that every segment of society is represented by a specific house or place. This may sound like the stock tool of most authors, but a closer look shows that Welty's use of place is more than that.

It is not always easy to show where a voice comes from. The character Welty created for her story 'Where Is the Voice Coming From?' is clearly a lower-class white Southerner (CS, pp. 603-607). He is a poor man who is jealous of a black man's success. By keeping us in his mind for long passages and by making us listen to the story in his own casual tone of voice, Welty shows us just where this man's voice comes from. The tragic event that inspired this short story was the killing of Medgar Evers in Jackson, Mississippi, on June 12, 1963. Medgar Evers, field secretary of the NAACP, was shot in the back with a 1917 Enfield rifle. Byron De La Beckwith was charged with the murder as his fingerprint was on the rifle. He grew up on a Greenwood plantation, rich in its Southern heritage, and his grandfather rode in the Confederate cavalry.[4] Two trials in 1964 ended with all-white juries deadlocked on verdicts, and Beckwith was not sentenced; but in December 1990 the now 70-year-old white supremacist is facing a new indictment for the same murder. As it turned out the man charged with the murder is not of a poor white family or neighbourhood, which only goes to show that fanatic racists can be in any part of society, a fact that does not detract from Welty's achievement in transforming an actual event into an imagined one while observing a clear distinction between fact and fiction. The social and political problems of her region are not the topics of her stories, and as she has said often, and most clearly in her essay 'Must the Novelist Crusade?' (1965) (ES, pp. 146-158), her fiction is not a platform for political opinions. If this story does appear to be closer to the actual event that inspired it than Welty's fiction is in general, the reason is probably its quick transmutation into art. The first version was written on the night of the murder (Con, p. 265). The story was created out of an emotional reaction to an act of perversion, and there was no time for a recollection in tranquillity. 'Where Is the Voice Coming From?' first appeared in the *New Yorker* on July 6, 1963; and the galleys for this publication are dated June 26, which is two weeks after the killing of Medgar Evers.[5]

The problems that preoccupy Welty in this story are particular to the place she describes, but they are finally universal in that the subject is our basic sense of right and wrong. The universal is brought to the story through the troubled mind of the main character, and it is the very convincing presence of his thoughts that saves the story from being mere propaganda. The situation speaks for itself without any crusading on the part of the author. The story is not a tract of social protest, it demonstrates how Welty even in the thick of the racial upheavals of the 1960s managed to write fiction that is 'stone deaf to argument'. If there is any message in this story, it goes beyond the political subtext and beyond the usual attack on conservative political and social traditions still ruling within some areas of the South in the early 1960s, for Welty also implies a rejection of the distortions and stereotypes aggressively imposed upon all Southern whites during that critical period of Southern history. In 1972 Eudora Welty summed up her reason for writing this story in an interview:

I had been having a feeling of uneasiness over the things being written about the South at that time, because most of them were done in other parts of the country and I thought most were synthetic. They were perfectly well-intentioned stories but generalities written from a distance to illustrate generalities. When that murder was committed, it suddenly crossed my consciousness that I knew what was in that man's mind because I'd lived all my life where it happened.

(Con, p. 83)

The voice of this man is the voice of one individual, one voice among many in Thermopylae but not a stock character; it is the voice of one man defending himself without much conviction. The political issues remain implicit, while the complexity of the situation and of people becomes the focus. Finally the existence of evil becomes more important than the dramatic events on a certain day in this Southern town, and only in this way does the story become art. The desired universality eventually has to be abstracted from the details of the life of a specific individual in a particular place, but the universality is achieved through specifying and particularizing. The important question for the writer must be: what does the thinking, acts, and fate of this man who deliberately kills mean to readers of another time and place? In this sense character is a more profound subject than situation and place. But place can have important and even dramatic significance, as it does in this story in which it is almost a character. It remains an 'almost', however, for Welty's interest in place leads to a more profound interest in the human being of that time and place. To understand that the murderer fails and tragically goes 'down, down, down' as a human being is ultimately more important than sensing where the murder is committed. And he knows he has failed completely; hence the constant elegiac note of his account.

In this short story the idea of place encompasses central concepts such as race, class, history and religion. It would be too much to ask to have all of these in the same paragraph, but most of the passages in Welty's 'Where Is the Voice Coming From?' bring out at least one or two of these central concerns through simple descriptions of place. One of the early paragraphs reads:

So you leave Four Corners and head west on Nathan B. Forrest Road, past the Surplus & Salvage, not much beyond the Kum Back Drive-In and Trailer Camp, not as far as where the signs start saying 'Live Bait', 'Used Parts', 'Fireworks', 'Peaches', and 'Sister Peebles Reader and Adviser'. Turn before you hit the city limits and duck back towards the I.C. tracks. And his street's been paved.

(CS, p. 603)

The voice we hear is that of a man who is on his way to a part of his home town of Thermopylae to commit a murder. He seems to take pleasure in his detailed knowledge of this part of town, and in his mind he goes over his route. Every detail is 'chosen, specific, pertinent, and thus revelatory', and the details reveal much about the potential killer. He is certainly not retarded, or even 'half-demented' as Peggy Prenshaw calls him,[6] he does not even appear to be unbalanced on the night of the murder, instead he seems cold-blooded, callous and fully aware of what he does; which is not, of course, proof that he fully understands why he is getting ready to kill. If his actions were accidental and the results of a disturbed mind, there would be no reason to ask where such a voice is coming from. It is essential that he seems as sane as most people. The places in town that he notices and enumerates tell us about his daily environment. It is a town where peaches are sold, it is possible to fish in the area, some people live in a trailer camp, at least two shops sell second hand articles, it is a town serviced by the Illinois Central railroad, there is enough superstition for a fortune teller to make a living, fireworks (for the July 4th celebration) can be sold here, probably unlike in some more restrictive community near by, and it is a place that has honoured General Nathan Bedford Forrest by naming a road for this Southern hero of the Civil War, who after Appomattox started the Ku Klux Klan (originally as a continued resistance movement). Although this is first and foremost a listing of what the Voice considers landmarks worth noticing, they also inform us about the town and the social situation there. In one sense the Voice and his town are one, their vocabulary and grammar are one: 'the Kum Back Drive In' and 'the signs start saying' are phrases of a kind. The Voice knows his way so well because he lives not too far from his victim, a black civil rights leader, and it is implied that this black neighborhood is where white men go to visit whores. But he does not live in the same neighborhood, and it is implied that housing districts are not integrated. The jealousy of the Voice and a part of his motivation are obvious in the last sentence of the quoted paragraph. He recognizes that the black couple in some financial and emotional ways are better off than he is, his background makes it impossible for him to accept the role of being inferior to black people. He is outraged: why should the street in a black man's neighborhood be paved when some whites, including the Voice, still live on dirt roads? So in one short paragraph and through a description of a part of a town we learn about the social and racial situation in Thermopylae, its historical background is implied, and the rest of the plot is foreshadowed through General Bedford Forrest's name, perhaps by the word 'Fireworks', and the mentioning of the paved street. Later we read that the black leader is shot and drops to 'his paved driveway'.

Eudora Welty makes sure the story is thoroughly located by mentioning that the rifle was fired from near a sassafras tree (a sweetgum in an earlier version) with a mockingbird busily mocking the assassin until the crack of the shot. The murder takes place at night between 3:45 a.m. and 4:35 a.m. and the temperature never drops below 92, the Voice sees both time and temperature on the sign of the local Branch Bank. His wife is sure he was bit by 'the skeeters'. The scorching heat of this night is in the rifle, the pavement, the truck keys, the doorknob, and the bed sheets. The heat is used by the author in her description of the relation between the Voice and his wife and by implication the relation between the assassin and the white society of Thermopylae. The Voice is a self-centred man who questions his own motives, but he does not like it when his spiteful and mocking wife tries to analyze his doings. He seems to be a bit henpecked; his wife certainly sits in judgment of him and his lack of faith in himself, and he wants her praise and acceptance. She wants to know why he has dropped the rifle at the scene of the crime:

And I told her, 'Because I'm so tired of ever'thing in the world being just that hot to the touch! The keys to the truck, the doorknob, the bedsheet, ever'thing, it's all like a stove lid. There just ain't much going that's worth holding on to it no more,' I says, 'when it's a hundred and two in the shade by day and by night not too much difference. I wish *you*'d laid *your* finger to that gun.'

(CS, p. 606)

Through the emphasis on the suffocating heat in Thermopylae, *thermae* appropriately meaning 'heat' in Greek, Welty manages to express the feverishly frustrated state of the assassin. He has been trying to 'hold on to something', but he is finding that it was not worth the effort. He obviously sees his wife as an extension of the society that in the media has called for the killing of the black leader and has brought the races to the point where it is too late to turn back from confrontation. A society which will not, as the Voice learns, celebrate its assassin, and the desired 'pat on the back' from the governor remains a fantasy. The Voice, who must be middle-aged, is deeply envious of the people who own their cars, live in North Thermopylae in houses with green grass, have garages with a light burning all night, and appear in the news. He himself has to borrow Buddy's, his brother-in-law's, truck to get to the black neighborhood. The following morning when he walks under the trees that, as he puts it poetically, hang 'them pones of bloom like split watermelon', it looks to him as if the town is on fire already, and he knows that the potential violence is in the town and its people: 'watch TV long enough and you'll see it all happen on Deacon Street in Thermopylae'. In its fear of change the town may choose to live up to its name and be a Thermopylae against the forced school integration of the time, but even though he speaks of 'us white people' the Voice does not kill for the rest of the town or for his wife. It is a mistake to see the Voice as simply a representative of a group of whites, who want to protect their status in society. The motives for this act of murder are even more basic and universal. Welty not only brings the town to life but also sees the town during a troubled period of its history, and this is convincingly done in remarks about columnists, TV, hundreds of cops, 'nigger children', American flags, Birmingham, Harlem and Chicago, Governor Ross Barnett, 'that nigger Meredith', 'it's still a free country', them Kennedys, and 'even the President so far, he can't walk in my house without being invited'. But what makes this story into art is not the perfect evocation of place and definite historical time, nor is it the obvious political subtext, it is the analysis of the universal nature of the Voice with all his serious flaws and total wrongheadedness. He killed, as he says, for his own 'pure D– satisfaction', he killed for bitterness and despair in an attempt to get rid of the load on his own shoulders. And this is where the voice really comes from. As Noel Polk has pointed out 'the voice comes from me, from such as me, from such as I know, from the character of the culture we all live in and have helped to create'.[7]

In his account of what happened the night of the murder the Voice is sensitive and creative like an artist. His grammar and syntax may often be incorrect, but in his creation of images and metaphors he is an artist. He describes the immediate effect of the fatal shot in these words: 'Something darker than him, like the wings of a bird, spread on his back and pulled him down. He climbed up once, like a man under bad claws, and like just blood could weigh a ton he walked with it on his back to better light. Didn't get no further than his door. And fell to stay' (CS, p. 604). This poetic paragraph has caused some consternation among the best Welty critics. Peggy Prenshaw finds that his narration 'detracts from the credibility of his characterization'.[8] And Ruth Vande Kieft finds that 'the killer seems suddenly too sensitive to his victim's vulnerability', and she admits that she is 'unwilling to believe that a man cowardly enough to shoot his helpless victim in the back would be capable of thinking of that victim humanely'.[9] These are serious reservations indeed for they argue the very heart of Welty's fiction. I believe that she wants to show the humanity of the assassin exactly because it is so hard to accept. If we deny him all human features, we will be repeating what *he* did in order to be able to kill, i.e. denying your victim all humanity in order to be able to hate. To reduce the Voice to a level less than human would defeat the purpose of warning us against man's inhumanity to man.

Only by accepting that even the killer is a human being can we begin to understand that his voice is a part of our voice and our responsibility. The Voice has great existential problems. For a while he manages to convince himself that he would be satisfied if he had what his victim enjoyed: a loving wife, a new white car, a good house with green grass and a paved driveway, a sense of achievement, and the applause of the world. The Voice is, of course, revealed in his interior monologue as a mass of prejudices and his thoughts are a study in frightening pride and nauseating vanity; but he is also a lonely and complex individual longing for recognition. The way he is able to move around uptown the day after the murder may indicate that he is unemployed; but he wants to be 'on top of the world' and he is willing to become the instrument of society for a moment if they will 'credit' him with the murder. He is even willing to risk capture. In an earlier version he states 'I ain't going to shy if they do come after me'.[10] In fact he seems to invite it when he leaves the rifle on the scene. He is a man who is proud that he has never once dropped, forgotten, lost or pawned his guitar for good and now he asks his wife to believe that he has accidentally dropped his rifle. He has, it seems, left his weapon on the scene as a clue, so he can be sure to be credited with this act of national importance. Wealth and popularity, the revered values of modern society, have escaped him, but he is a product of the pursuit of them. Now he hopes for recognition and perhaps popularity through the murder of a carefully selected victim, who can serve as a scapegoat for both the Voice and his town. He is proud when a $500 reward is offered in the case, and he calmly anticipates the possibility of frying in the electric chair. He is a man who is tired of being a 'no 'count' who never even had a photo made of himself, and now he wants the attention that has eluded him his whole life (except when his mother told him to come home once through an ad in the county weekly). His parents, who might have paid attention to him, are merely memories of the past, his wife does not think much of him, and although he appears to be a church-going man (from the way he remembers a shouting preacher's eyeballs), he does not go there now that he needs help. The thin streak of humanity that there is in the assassin is that through a desperate act of self-assertion he wants to be recognized, accepted, credited, or just noticed by the society whose values have made him feel inferior. But as his wife points out, the joke is on him. The news is still full of pictures of his victim, nobody knows the Voice and he receives no publicity. The local seller of roasted peanuts tells him: 'They'll never find him', and the Voice knows that everybody is still better off than he is and that 'you can't win'. When we last see him he is alone, in his isolation he tries to take comfort in the fact that he is 'evermore the one' and that he has seen his victim fall down, but it does not comfort him. He takes his guitar and starts to play the blues monotonously and depressively, his separateness has become his curse, and finally he is the one who is 'down, down, down'.

Place offers a more lasting identity, and the Voice has an identity that is attached to and shaped by his place. But his restless existential search for acceptance, however misguided and atrocious, is finally of any place and of all time. But it is only through Eudora Welty's familiarity with this particular place that the particular voice becomes universal. The manuscripts of this story, which are on deposit with the Mississippi Department of Archives and History in Jackson, offer thirteen other working titles. They span from 'ask me my daddy's name', 'find me', and 'it was me' to 'where is the racket coming from?' and 'voice from an unknown interior'. A fairly complete manuscript is called 'From the unknown', and this seems to have been Miss Welty's favourite title for some time. The choice of the final title, which is a question to the reader, is a marked improvement over the others. The question of the title is answered during a reading of the story. As indicated by other discarded titles: 'a voice from the Jackson interior' and 'from my room', Welty chose not to use the word 'unknown' in her final title because she knows very well where this voice comes from. The story reads as a broad accusation: Welty slowly lets her reader discover that the whole society of Thermopylae, present and past, is responsible for the death of the black leader. The voice is *not* unknown to the author or to us, we hear it all of our lives; it is a universal voice of petty jealousy, paranoid prejudice and inhumanity to others that we all run the risk of falling victim to now and again. We know the voice well, it is an everyday presence in our neighborhood.

NOTES

1. Eudora Welty, *The Collected Stories* (New York: Harcourt Brace Jovanovich, 1980), p. 621; hereafter cited in the text as CS.
2. Eudora Welty, *Conversations*, ed. Peggy W. Prenshaw (Jackson: University Press of Mississippi, 1984), p. 281; hereafter cited in the text as Con.
3. Eudora Welty, *The Eye of the Story: Selected Essays and Reviews* (New York: Random House, 1978), pp. 116-133; hereafter cited in the text as ES.

4. *The Clarion-Ledger*, Jackson, Mississippi, Dec. 18, 1990, p. 9A.
5. Suzanne Marrs, *The Welty Collection* (Jackson: University Press of Mississippi, 1988), p. 50.
6. Peggy W. Prenshaw, *A Study of Setting in the Fiction of Eudora Welty* (Ann Arbor: University Microfilms International, 1970), p. 100.
7. Noel E. Polk, 'Continuity and Change in Eudora Welty's "Where Is the Voice Coming From?" and "The Demonstrators"', *Turning Points*, Mississippi Mindscape (Jackson: Mississippi Committee for the Humanities, 1986), p. 8.
8. Prenshaw, *A Study of Setting*, p. 101.
9. Ruth N. Vande Kieft, '"Where Is the Voice Coming From?": Teaching Eudora Welty', *Eudora Welty: Eye of the Storyteller*, ed. Dawn Trouard (Kent State University Press, 1989), p. 200.
10. Eudora Welty, 'From the Unknown', in John Kuehl, ed., *Write and Rewrite: A Study of the Creative Process* (New York: Meredith Press, 1967), pp. 4-14, p. 12.

Lost in the Cosmos:
Place in Walker Percy

Karl-Heinz Westarp

To be born and to live is to be dislocated.
Blaise Pascal

When Walker Percy died on May 10th, 1990, 74 years old, he had lived for 40 years in a house near Covington, Louisiana, overlooking a peaceful bayou some 40 kilometers north of New Orleans. Born in Birmingham, Alabama, he moved at the age of 15, after his father's suicide and his mother's fatal car accident, to live in the care of his uncle William Alexander Percy in Greenville, Mississippi. After graduating as a chemistry major from North Carolina in 1937, he studied medicine at Columbia, S.C., where he got his M.D. in 1941. The only periods Percy spent in the North were his internship as an autopsist at Bellevue Hospital, New York, between 1941 and 1942, and the subsequent three-year stay in a sanatorium overlooking Saranac Lake in the Adirondacks, N.Y., where he was treated for tuberculosis, contracted during his internship. The South is where he felt at home - which doesn't mean that he uncritically accepted or defended its values; the South is his 'somewhere', the place that fostered and nourished his imagination as it did the works of his contemporaries Flannery O'Connor, Eudora Welty and William Faulkner, the master of place in modern American fiction. In a World Net interview transmitted in 1986 he said:

> I am a Southern writer in the sense that I depend on my Southern background for the decor, the setting, the sense of place which any novelist must have. ... I am not a typical example of a Southern writer ... I owe less to Faulkner and Southern writers and indeed American writers than to certain French writers: to be specific, Jean-Paul Sartre, Albert Camus, Gabriel Marcel, and to go back a way, Blaise Pascal.[1]

Indeed, all his novels, *The Moviegoer* (1955), *The Last Gentleman* (1966), *Love in the Ruins* (1971), *Lancelot* (1977), *The Second Coming* (1980) and *The Thanatos Syndrome* (1987), are set exclusively in the South, except the first part of *The Last Gentleman*, which takes place in and around New York's Central Park. In his 1981 interview with Jan Nordby Gretlund, Percy has a revealing comment on the South:

> The South has a greater sense of place than other parts of the country; but the South is changing. The South is more like the rest of the country now. ... The South is going through the process of losangelization. That's not good. The trick is, given the New South, which is not the South of Faulkner, not the South of Eudora, it is not the South of Flannery, it is the South of Interstate 12 and Highway 190. It is the South of Los Angeles. How to humanize that! How do you live with that? What I am trying to do is to figure out how a man can come to himself, living in a place like that.[2]

Percy's Southern settings have caused him to be classified in critical terms as a regional writer, in itself a concept not easily defendable, because every fiction has its very own and detailed setting. Percy makes it quite clear that he uses setting for much wider purposes: 'It would be impossible for me to write as I do unless I were a Southerner. One is simply stuck with one's place, and God help you if you're not. ... I'm not interested in the particular mythos and mystique of the South. I have other concerns. I simply use the Southern experience to serve my novelistic concerns' (Con, p. 219). Also for Flannery O'Connor, whom Walker Percy admired as an artist, the concrete Southern setting 'is a gateway to reality',[3] enabling her to read 'a small history in a universal light' (MM, p. 58) or as John Dewey has strikingly formulated it, 'The local is the only universal, upon that all art builds'.[4] O'Connor thought that 'The writer operates at a peculiar crossroads where time and place and eternity somehow meet. His problem is to find that location' (MM, p. 59). Eudora Welty, the other Southern writer whom Percy held in great respect, supports Percy and O'Connor's views on place in her splendid essay on 'Place in Fiction' (1956): 'Fiction depends for its life on place. Location is the crossroads of circumstance, the proving ground of "What happened? Who's here? Who's coming?" ... Place in fiction is the named, identified, concrete, exact and exacting, and therefore credible, gathering spot of all that has been felt, is about to be experienced, in the novel's progress'.[5]

Place meticulously detailed, then, is not just a backdrop to a story, it is an essential door into its narrative universe. The following two examples show Walker Percy's characteristic presentation of place. First Barrett's ironic description of Central Park in *The Last Gentleman*:

> It was a beautiful day but only after the fashion of beautiful days in New York. The sky was no more than an ordinary Eastern sky, mild and blue and hazed over, whitened under the blue and of not much account. It was a standard sky by which

all other skies are measured. As for the park, green leaves or not, it belonged to the animal kingdom rather than the vegetable. It had a zoo smell. Last summer's grass was as coarse and yellow as lion's hair and worn bare in spots, exposing the tough old hide of the earth. The tree trunks were polished. Bits of hair clung to the bark as if a large animal had been rubbing against them. Nevertheless, thought he, it is a good thing to see a park put to good hard use by millions of people, used and handled in its every square inch like a bear garden.[6]

Though he has a remarkable feel for the place, one senses throughout that Barrett does not belong here and that his feeling of dislocation has deeper dimensions than the purely geographical. As Percy said in connection with Binx Bolling, the protagonist of *The Moviegoer*, his 'dislocation in space is real. ... But the dislocation in space is a symbol or an objective correlative of his real dislocation, and his real dislocation has to do with a dislocation from the ordinary modes of existence in America; ... He is dislocated, he is an exile from his own traditions' (WN). Most of Percy's protagonists are 'in some sense or other more or less dislocated, alienated, deracinated' (WN). In the opening section of *The Second Coming* Percy describes one of Will Barrett's odd and deeply disturbing experiences:

Once again he found himself in the pretty reds and yellows of the countryside. As he drove along a gorge, he suffered another spell. Again the brilliant sunlight grew dim. Light seemed to rise from the gorge. He slowed, turned on the radio, and tried to tune in a nonreligious program. He could not find one. In the corner of his eye a dark bird flew through the woods, keeping pace with him. He knew what to do.

Pulling off at an overlook, he took the Luger from the glove compartment of the Mercedes. As he stepped out, he caught sight of a shadowy stranger in the mirror fixed to the door. But he quickly saw that the stranger was himself. The reason the figure appeared strange was that it was reflected by two mirrors, one the rearview mirror, the other the dark windowglass of the Mercedes door.

He smiled. Yes, that was it. With two mirrors it is possible to see oneself briefly as a man among men rather than a self sucking everything into itself.[7]

I have quoted this large extract to show how Percy uses the concrete setting as a means to an end; Barrett fails to recognize himself, fore-shadowing the dramatic change that is going to happen to him in the course of the novel. In Percy's case the concreteness of place bears an often conscious stamp of universality because of his explicit interest and studies in linguistics, psychology, philosophy and theology. Before he started writing novels Percy published essays on linguistic, medical and philosophical topics, addressing himself to the mystery of language and man's triadic cognitive structure, which he calls the Delta factor or 'the arrival of man himself and his breakthrough into the daylight of language and consciousness and knowing'.[8] As late as in his Jefferson Lecture, delivered on May 3, 1989, and entitled 'The Fateful Rift: The San Andreas Fault in the Modern Mind', Percy adduces Charles Sanders Peirce's (1839-1914) pioneer thinking in this context. 'Peirce saw that the one way to get at it, the great modern rift between mind and matter, was the only place where they intersect, language. ... The copula "is", spoken or implied, is nothing less than the tiny triadic lever that moves the entire world into the reach of our peculiar species'.[9] Walker Percy constantly tried to come to grips with the human situation of alienation and in line with Kierkegaard and Sartre launched an attack upon the sciences, in particular the radical insufficiency of B.F. Skinner's behavioral explanation of man and of Noam Chomsky's approach to the uniquely human phenomenon of language. In the Jefferson Lecture Percy stated, 'our view of the world, which we get consciously or unconsciously from modern science, is radically incoherent' (TFR, p. 1). The formulation is stronger and more explicit in *Lost in the Cosmos*: 'How can an immanent theory of evolution mounted from the transcending posture of science account for the appearance in the Cosmos of a triumphant, godlike, murderous alien, the only alien in the Cosmos, Homo sapiens sapiens, e.g., the scientist himself?'[10] Percy's decision to present his philosophical ideas not only in scholarly treatises but as integral parts of his novels accounts for the high level of learning and complexity in his fiction. Walker Percy's philosophical fiction has puzzled many readers, who have found his writings a sometimes excruciating challenge. In a 1966 interview Percy explained his position as philosopher and novelist:

I use the fiction form as a vehicle for incarnating ideas, as did Jean Paul Sartre and Gabriel Marcel. I long ago decided that my philosophy is in the vein of the existentialist, as theirs were. Both said that fiction is not just recreation. In my case, it is the embodiment of ideas of both philosophy and psychiatry into a form through which the reader can see a concept which otherwise might not be recognized.

(Con, p. 9)

Percy depicts Binx Bolling, Will Barrett, Dr. More and his other protagonists as wayfarers through a very concrete world on a quest for the true self which can only be reached by suffering the throes of indirection, typical of human existence defined by the prior cognitive frameworks of time and place. In an interview with Carlton Cremeens (1968) he said: 'Man is alienated by the nature of his being here. He is here as a stranger and as a pilgrim, which is the way alienation is conceived in my books. ... He is *Homo viator*' (Con, pp. 28-29). Percy does not deny that this view of man is deeply influenced by his Catholic thinking. 'To me, the Catholic view of man as pilgrim, in transit, in journey, is very compatible with the vocation of a novelist because a novelist is writing about man in transit, man as pilgrim', he confessed in 1971 in an interview with John C. Carr (Con, p. 64).

In the following I should like to focus on Percy's presentation of man's place in the world in his two non-fictional works *The Message in the Bottle, How Queer Man Is, How Queer Language Is, and What One Has to Do with the Other* (1975), which is a collection of linguistic/philosophical essays, and *Lost in the Cosmos, The Last Self-Help Book* (1983), which is Percy's most consistently satiric depiction of modern man's paradoxical shortcomings. In the title essay of *The Message in the Bottle*, which I have chosen for further analysis, place is not as concrete as in the above-mentioned examples from Percy's fiction: in keeping with the scholarly argumentative language place is described in a general or abstract way, similar to Samuel Beckett's stage directions in *Waiting for Godot*: 'ACT I *A country road. A tree. Evening*'.[11] The opening paragraph of 'The Message in the Bottle' runs as follows:

Suppose a man is a castaway on an island. He is, moreover, a special sort of cast-away. He has lost his memory in the shipwreck and has no recollection of where came from or who he is. All he knows is that one day he finds himself cast up on the beach. But it is a pleasant place ... The castaway, ... forms the habit of taking a walk on the beach early in the morning. Here he regularly comes upon bottles which have been washed up by the waves.

(MB, pp. 119-120)

It is important to notice that Percy talks about a castaway on an island, i.e. not a particular character in a particular place but a man on an isolated island. The bottles contain a single message each, and the man is interested in finding out where the bottles come from and what messages they contain. The central argument about the kind of messages contained in the bottles advances in a syllogistic way and reaches its conclusion *per modum exclusionis*. The castaway sees a basic distinction between on the one hand messages consisting of sentences communicating knowledge *sub specie æternitatis* or which are general, verifiable because repeatable, truths and on the other hand sentences containing news which is historical and not repeatable but which can also be submitted to a process of verification/falsification. In connection with news this process is only possible, however, if adequate action is taken upon reception of the news and prior to the verifying procedure. For example, you can only verify the message that there is food in the house next door by going there. The castaway is in a predicament of existential homelessness and anxiety, he is 'a stranger who is in the world but who is not at home in the world' (MB, p. 142), who 'is alienated by the

112

nature of his being here' (Con, pp. 28-29). Because of his predicament as an amnesic castaway it is an essential part of his existence that he is always 'in search for news from across the seas' (MB, pp. 139, 140, 144), which he hopes to be significant messages of vital importance in relation to his origin and his present predicament. The castaway finding himself in the predicament of 'the Jasperian notion of shipwrecked man, Heidegger's notion of ... Geworfenheit' (MB, p. 146)[12] will, confronted with news from across the seas 'be a fool or a knave if he did not heed the news' (MB, p. 136). He will follow the invitation 'Come'.

There is little doubt that Percy here uses the form of the parable to communicate his view of the human situation. At the end it becomes clear, I think, that this essay is nothing less than a veiled theology of the Revelation. In spite of its scientific form this essay is more openly 'apostolic' than any other of Percy's works. The shipwrecked castaway on an island, amnesic of his origin, finding bottled messages on the beach is Percy's image of fallen man on earth who has forgotten his relation to God in spite of numerous God-sent messages and messengers.

Figure 1.

How the Problematic Self can Escape its Predicament by Science

AB = The problematic self, finding itself in a disappointing world and in all manner of difficult relationships, escapes by joining the scientific community, either by becoming a scientist or by understanding science.

BC = The transcending community of scientists.

CD = From the perspective of BC, the world can now be seen by A triumphantly as a dyadic system.

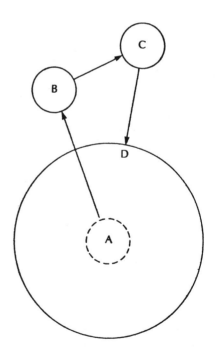

The same idea of having lost our sense of place also pervades Percy's last book of non-fiction. *Lost in the Cosmos* is again about man in general, and about his habitat between centre and periphery is the cosmos, about which he knows increasingly more; yet he is in danger of losing his 'self', or has already lost it. In 1984 Percy said to Jo Gulledge: 'But notice that there is a curious movement taking place while you're explaining the whole world by dyadic theory: you yourself are getting more and more removed from it' (Con, p. 297). Walker Percy shows this position characteristic of 'the problematical self' in Diagram 14, LC, p. 115 (see figure 1).

Lost in the Cosmos is an encyclopedic inventory and leaves no area of late twentieth century knowledge and experience untouched by Percy's caustic intelligence. The multiple-choice title of the book, the short preliminary quiz – 'If you can answer these questions you are not lost in the Cosmos' (LC, p. 9) and don't need to read the rest of the book – and the 'Twenty-Question Multiple-Choice Self-Help Quiz' ending with the two science-fiction 'Space Odysseys' make fun of our quiz mania, our space-age expectations and our computerized multiple-choice form of knowledge. In all there are six different titles to choose from, all hinting at man's position in the cosmos.

> The Strange Case of the Self, your Self, the Ghost which Haunts the Cosmos ... Why it is that of all the billions and billions of strange objects in the Cosmos – novas, quasars, pulsars, black holes – you are beyond doubt the strangest ... How it is possible for the man who designed Voyager 19, which arrived at Titania, a satellite of Uranus, three seconds off schedule and a hundred yards off course after a flight of six years, to be one of the most screwed-up creatures in California – or the Cosmos.
>
> (LC, pp. 7-8)

Using material and themes he used before, Percy is careful always to focus attention upon our various forms of self-deception: we indulge in knowing vast numbers of details about the physical data of the cosmos, including man. Percy hammers in the message: 'How you can survive in the Cosmos about which you know more and more while knowing less and less about yourself' (LC, p. 1). 'The lost self: Every advancement in an objective understanding of the Cosmos and in its technological control further distances the self from the Cosmos precisely in the degree of the advance – so that in the end the self becomes a space-bound ghost which roams the very Cosmos it understands perfectly' (LC, p. 17).

Percy's interest is clearly to describe the situation of the self and assist in the self-finding process.[13] He is concerned about the position of being lost in the cosmos with 'no news of how you got into such a fix or how to get out – or the even more preposterous eventuality that news did come from the God of the Cosmos, who took pity on your ridiculous plight and entered the space and time of your insignificant planet to tell you something' (LC, p. 81). In the opening quiz Percy presents the choice between eleven different kinds of consciousness of self, among them

(a) The cosmological self. The self is either unconscious of itself or only conscious of it self insofar as it is identified with a cosmological or classificatory system, e.g. totemism. Ask a Bororo tribesman: Who are you? He may reply: I am a parakeet. (Ask an L.S.U. fan at a football game: Who are you? He may reply: I am a tiger.)
(LC, p. 15)

(g) The lost self. With the passing of cosmological myths and the fading of Christianity as a guarantor of the identity of the self, the self becomes dislocated.
(LC, p. 17)

In the course of the 'Twenty-Question Multiple-Choice Self-Help Quiz' (LC, p. 19) space is omnipresent in a great variety of concretized places, always related to the problems of the self, which seems to be 'misplaced' (LC, p. 40), 'nowhere' (LC, p. 30) and Crusoe-like 'would like to discover his place in the Cosmos, discover a man Friday, or failing that, at least teach goats to talk' (LC, p. 169).

In the 'Intermezzo' Percy develops 'A short history of the Cosmos with Emphasis on the Nature and Origin of the Self, ... or Why it is Possible to feel Bad in a Good Environment and Good in a Bad Environment' (LC, p. 86), – an experience shared by the two commuters described in 'The Message in the Bottle' (MB, p. 134). In this 'semiotic primer of the self' Percy describes a short history of nature and of the origin of self, 'despite its offhand tone, as serious as can be' (Con, p. 285). Again Percy adduces the Delta factor or man's discovery of the sign as the disctinctively human activity (LC, p. 94; cp. Con, p. 177), which is social in origin and elevates man's world above all other organisms' dyadic environment. Yet man has experienced a 'catastrophe of the self', which, semiotically, is 'the banishment of the self-conscious self from its own world of signs' (LC, p. 108). This is the reason for man's radical alienation, his being lost in the Cosmos. Percy's conception of man's original position in the Cosmos is clearly shown in diagram no. 12 'I am a self with you under God' (LC, p. 112) or, as he expressed it in an interview with Charles T. Bunting in 1971: 'The only way the self can become self is by becoming itself transparently before God' (Con, p. 49).

The self becomes itself by recognizing God as a spirit, creator of the Cosmos and therefore of one's self as a creature but a creature nonetheless, who shares with a community of like creatures the belief that God transcends the entire Cosmos and has actually entered human history – or will enter it – in order to redeem man from the catastrophe which has over taken his self.

(LC, p. 112)

The basic appeal of Lost in the Cosmos is the age-old imperative known from an inscription in the temple at Delphi: *Gnoti Seauton*, Know Thyself! It is revealing that Percy after the publication of the book decided in the paperback edition to balance Nietzsche's agnostic epigraph 'We are unkown, we knowers, to ourselves' with St. Augustine's 'O God, I pray you let me know my self'. Through this Percy seems to indicate his despair of man's ability to reach self-knowledge, yet at the same time his hope that it may be offered to us through a message 'from across the seas', to use his expression from 'The Message in the Bottle'.

Percy is 'aware of the necessity to shock the reader out of self-unawareness and into recognition of the advanced derangement of the world' (LC, p. 152) both through these texts and in his fiction. He appeals to us to continue our search for the self, to find its place in the cosmos. An acceptance of man's predicament in the cosmos is a presupposition for further steps in the direction of anagnorisis, of finding the self in its right place.

NOTES

1. 'One to One with Walker Percy', World Net Interview, (December 3, 1986); hereafter abbreviated in the text as WN.
2. Lewis A. Lawson & Victor A. Kramer, eds., *Conversations With Walker Percy*, (Jackson: University Press of Mississippi, 1985), p. 214; hereafter abbreviated in the text as Con.
3. Robert & Sally Fitzgerald, eds., *Flannery O'Connor, Mystery and Manners* (New York: Farrar, Straus & Giroux, 1962), p. 54; hereafter abbreviated in the text as MM.
4. Quoted in Frederick Turner, *The Spirit of Place* (Sierra Club, 1990), p. 297.
5. Eudora Welty, *The Eye of the Story* (New York: Random House, 1978), pp. 118 and 122.
6. Walker Percy, *The Last Gentleman* (New York: Farrar, Straus & Giroux, 1966), p. 12.
7. Walker Percy, *The Second Coming* (New York: Washington Square Press, 1981), p. 15.
8. Walker Percy, *The Message in the Bottle* (New York: Farrar, Straus & Giroux, 1971), p. 3; hereafter abbreviated in the text as MB.

9. Walker Percy, 'The Fateful Rift: The San Andreas Fault in the Modern Mind', released by Facts, (Washington: National Endowment for the Humanities, May 3, 1989), pp. 13, 16; hereafter abbreviated in the text as TFR.

10. Walker Percy, *Lost in the Cosmos: The Last Self-Help Book* (New York: Washington Square Press, 1984), p. 163; hereafter abbreviated in the text as LC.

11. Samuel Beckett, *Waiting for Godot* (London: Faber & Faber, 1956), p. 7.

12. 'Percy once described the world in which he lives as "a dark place ... a kind of desert, a bombed-out place ... of blasted trees and barbed wire"'. Quoted in *The Harper American Literature*, vol 2 (New York: Harper & Row, 1987), p. 2027.

13. Paul Ricoeur uses the concept 'self-understanding' and distinguishes between the self which emerges from the understanding of a text and the ego which precedes this understanding. *Hermeneutics and the Human Sciences*, ed. John B. Thompson (Cambridge: Cambridge University Press, 1981), p. 193.

Notes on Contributors

Darlene E. Erickson, Ph.D. is an Assistant Professor at Ohio Dominican College in Columbus, Ohio. Erickson's current major research interest is the work of the American poet Marianne Moore. She has the manuscript of a book about Moore entitled *Illusion is More Precise than Precision: The Poetry of Marianne Moore* in the hands of the University of Alabama Press. Erickson has taught at Ohio State University and at Miami University, Oxford, Ohio.

Richard E. Fisher is an Associate Professor of American Cultural Studies at the English Department, Lund University, Sweden. His publications include articles on American literature (Melville, Faulkner, Native American writers, Updike) and collaborations on (or contributions to) books including an American slang dictionary, an introduction to American literature (for Swedish high schools), a Swedish radio/TV correspondence course in university English, and the culture chapter in a Swedish University textbook on American Studies.

Jan Nordby Gretlund is an Associate Professor of American literature at Odense University, Denmark. He is a contributor to *American Literary Scholarship* and co-editor of *Realist of Distances: Flannery O'Connor Revisited* and *Walker Percy: Novelist and Philosopher.*

David Kranes was born in Boston and is presently a Professor of English and Theater at the University of Utah. He is a writer of plays, novels, screenplays and short stories, and his third novel, *The Hunting Years*, was published in 1984. He is Artistic Director of the Sundance Institute's Playwrights' Lab.

Patrick Lane was born in Nelson, British Columbia, 1939. His thirteen adult poetry collections include *Poems, New and Selected* (Oxford, 1978), *The Measure* (Black Moss, 1980), *Old Mother* (Oxford, 1981), *A Linen Row, A Caftan Magpie* (Thistledown, 1985), *Selected Movies* (Oxford, 1987), and *Winter* (Regina, Saskatchewan, 1990), several of which have won prestigeous literary awards. Patrick Lane presently teaches at the University of Saskatchewan, Saskatoon, Canada.

James I. McClintock is Distinguished Professor of English, American Studies, and Science-Technology Studies at Michigan State University, where he is Director of the American Studies Program. His publications include *White Logic: a Critical Study of Jack London's Short Stories;* articles on contemporary American writers such as Thomas Pynchon and E.L. Doctorow; articles on nature essayists such as Annie Dillard, Joseph Wood Krutch, and Edward Abbey; and other articles relating to science and American cultural history.

Ellen W. Munley is an Associate Professor of French and Comparative Literature at Regis College, near Boston. Her scholarly articles include an in-depth study of narrative strategies in Nathalie Sarraute's work, published in *Contemporary Literature.* She has also written and delivered a wide range of papers on foreign language pedagogy and feminist criticism. She is currently working on a book exploring inscriptions of gender in contemporary fiction in France and in North and South America.

Regine Rosenthal received her Ph.D. (1982) from the University of München, where she taught American and comparative literature until 1990. Presently she teaches American literature at the University of Augsburg, Germany. In 1985 she was a Fellow at the Salzburg Seminar. Her main field of interest is Jewish American literature and comparative aspects thereof. She has also published a monograph on the picaresque novel.

Joseph C. Schöpp, Professor of American Studies at the University of Hamburg, Germany, is the author of a monograph on Allen Tate (1975) and numerous articles on American literature. His latest publication *Ausbruch aus der Mimesis* (1990) discusses innovative narrative strategies in the postmodern American novel. He is currently working on a book about travelogues as forms of cultural exploration.

Karl-Heinz Westarp is an Associate Professor of English and American Literature at the University of Aarhus, Denmark. He has published articles on Joyce and on authors of the American South; he has edited a collection of essays on Joyce (1983) and co-edited volumes on British Drama in the Eighties (1986), on Flannery O'Connor (1987) and on Walker Percy (1991). His extended studies in O'Connor manuscripts are presently being prepared for publication under the title *The Growing Craft*, a synoptic variorum edition of her 'Judgement Day' material.